MW00445346

POWER STUDIES 1

CONTENTS

Page		Audio Track

Hal Leonard Publishing Corporation
7777 West Bluemound Road P.O. Box 13819 Milwaukee, WI 53213

POWER STUDIES 1

INTRODUCTION

The *Power Studies* series is designed to bring you countless hours of musical enjoyment while enhancing the learning process and building your chops. In *Power Studies*, you are presented with an exciting array of your favorite songs to hone your musicianship and supplement the concepts in the *Wolf Marshall Guitar Method*. This will provide you with a meaningful environment for applying the method ideas while developing a working repertoire. An environment which is stimulating and fun—in the context of real music.

Through the music itself, you will experience and assimilate the same powerful ideas that have inspired all the great guitarists from Jimi Hendrix and Eric Clapton to Stevie Ray Vaughan and Edward Van Halen. The *Power Studies* material is a varied collection embracing many styles of music while focusing on a tight core of must-know tunes. Besides the emphasis on rock classics you'll explore different styles like rockabilly, blues, fusion, country, heavy metal and pop. Each *Power Studies* song is purposefully selected to reflect and amplify the important guitar playing principles found in your corresponding *Wolf Marshall Guitar Method*. You will get to know the music on a very intimate level.

Every song is preceded by a full annotation and performance notes which amount to a complete guitar lesson in their own right. These sections are filled with musical insights and shed light on the important technical points within each composition. You'll learn about the professional application of chords, scales, articulations, song form, rhythm playing, arpeggios and much more. Above all, *Power Studies* is dedicated to you— playing, hearing and understanding the music you love.

THE RECORDING

The recording for this book contains all of the songs from the book in complete musical settings. The featured guitar part (found in gray box areas in the book) is on the right channel, the rest of the instrumentation is on the left channel. The use of the gray box areas is not employed in songs where there is only one guitar part featured. Most of the time, the featured part contains material that explores the concepts and techniques taught in *Basics 1* of the *Wolf Marshall Guitar Method*. Occasionally, when there is only one guitar in an arrangement, the featured guitar part may go beyond the *Basics 1* level.

Wolf Marshall — guitars
Gary Ferguson — drums, percussion
Michael Della Gala — bass
John Nau — keyboards
Warren Hamm — harmonica on "Hoochie Coochie Man"
Michael McCarty — additional sythesizer, percussion & engineer
Produced by Wolf Marshall

FOREWORD

In preparing these *Power Studies*, one naturally faces the dilemma of finding the ideal songs as musical illustrations to support the various teaching points as they are presented in *Basics 1*. However songs don't always cooperate with authors. They are living, breathing musical entities which yield techniques and theory only after existing as art. And that's as it should be.

With that said, there seemed two ways to approach the matter. One was to present only the pieces of a song which reflected the "letter of the lesson." In other words, omitting sections beyond the immediate scope of a lesson to satisfy teaching criteria alone. This approach would result in butcheries like songs without solos and often without some of their most significant riffs. Can you imagine "Crossroads" without its immortal Clapton solo? Or Metallica's "The Unforgiven" minus the signature fingerpicked intro? Unthinkable. Instead an alternate route was chosen. In the *Power Studies* series you play the entire song with all its parts intact to form a complete musical picture.

In the performance notes at the beginning of each song you will find points which are cross-referenced to other *Wolf Marshall Guitar Method* volumes. For example, references to certain lead guitar playing techniques, scales and concepts from *Basics 2* or *Basics 3* may be cited in the performance notes of *Power Studies 1*. These will aid you in not only selecting the particular "graded" parts to play within the *Power Studies 1* course but will provide the advancing guitarist with a continuum of music throughout the *Power Studies* series.

By presenting each song in its entirety, complete with annotations, each volume of the series is as viable and valuable as the next and consequently no vital step in your musical growth will be overlooked or slighted. There is another benefit. The extra motivation it takes an aspiring guitarist to rise above his present abilities and struggle to learn a trickier scale fingering or that more difficult chord may well be what makes him a dedicated player and ultimately a successful musician. In this spirit I can truly say that this series lives up to its name—*Power Studies!*

Wolf Marshall

POWER STUDIES 1 BONUS SONG LIST

A list of songs not appearing in this volume that make use of techniques and concepts found in specific chapters of *Basics 1* of the *Wolf Marshall Guitar Method*.

Basics 1, Chapters One/Two – Open Power Chords

1. Whole Lotta Rosie—AC/DC
2. My Head's In Mississippi—Z.Z.Top
3. Barracuda—Heart
4. Cat Scratch Fever—Ted Nugent
5. Dirty Deeds—AC/DC
6. Walk Softly On This Heart Of Mine—Kentucky Headhunters
7. Young Lust—Aerosmith
8. Domino—Kiss
9. Summertime Blues—The Who
10. Houses Of The Holy—Led Zeppelin
11. Night Train—Guns N' Roses
12. Bottoms Up—Van Halen
13. Big Bad Moon—Joe Satriani
14. Man In The Box—Alice In Chains
15. I Love Rock And Roll—Joan Jett

Basics 1, Chapters Three/Five – Riffs

1. Lady Madonna—The Beatles
2. Baby Lee—John Lee Hooker/Robert Cray
3. Crossfire—Stevie Ray Vaughan
4. Runnin' Down A Dream—Tom Petty
5. Oh Pretty Woman—Roy Orbison/Van Halen
6. Open All Night—Georgia Satellites
7. Given The Dog A Bone—AC/DC
8. Rattlesnake Shake—Skid Row
9. Honey Don't—Carl Perkins/The Beatles
10. Love In An Elevator—Aerosmith
11. Guitar Boogie Shuffle—Arthur Smith/The Virtues
12. Falling To Pieces—Faith No More
13. Through The Never—Metallica
14. Savoy—Jeff Beck
15. Hideaway—Jeff Healey/Freddie King

Basics 1, Chapter Four – 12-bar Blues/ Blues Comping

1. Rock And Roll—Led Zeppelin
2. Rock And Roll Music—Chuck Berry/The Beatles
3. Everybody's Trying To Be My Baby—Carl Perkins/The Beatles
4. Close To You—Stevie Ray Vaughan/Willie Dixon
5. Same Ol' Situation—Motley Crue
6. Rock And Roll Ain't Noise Pollution—AC/DC
7. My Girl—Aerosmith
8. Rhythm Of Love—Yes
9. Gypsy Road—Cinderella
10. Life By The Drop—Stevie Ray Vaughan
11. Lookin' Out A Window—Stevie Ray Vaughan
12. Keep Your Hands To Yourself—Georgia Satellites
13. Sweet Home Alabama—Lynyrd Skynyrd
14. Before You Accuse Me—Eric Clapton
15. Rocker—AC/DC

Basics 1, Chapter Six/Seven – Minor Sounds/Minor Pentatonic Scale/String Bending

1. Scuttle Buttin'—Stevie Ray Vaughan
2. Baby Please Don't Go—Them
3. Pipeline—The Chantays/Stevie Ray Vaughan
4. Smoking Gun—Robert Cray
5. Roadhouse Blues—The Doors
6. Wham—Lonnie Mack/Stevie Ray Vaughan
7. Little Sister—Elvis Presley
8. Big Block—Jeff Beck
9. Finish What Ya Started—Van Halen
10. That'll Be The Day—Buddy Holly

BIRTHDAY
The Beatles

This late-Sixties classic was written spontaneously by the Beatles in the studio for their *White Album*. Built on a driving repeated melody, this is a perfect example of a riff-based rock tune. (See *Basics 1*: Ch. 3.)

The main riff is played ensemble—a composite of Gtr. 1 and Gtr. 2 (plus bass guitar which doubles the melody of Gtr. 1), Riff A and Riff B respectively (reputedly both played by John Lennon). Let's focus on Gtr. 2's part, Riff B. This figure, heard in the intro [A], verse [B], interlude [E] and coda [F], is moved through the chord progression of a 12-bar blues in A (*Basics 1*: Ch. 4). Note the use of I, IV and V chord numerals under the riff. See (*Basics 1*: Ch. 5.)

Visualize the three main riff patterns as sharing the same shape, based on A5, D5 and E5 power chords, but having different roots. Be aware of two phrasing details in the riff: palm-muting (*Basics 1*: p. 27) and the hand sliding into position (*Basics 3*).

Gtr.1 is the lead part which is a movable riff (*Basics 2*: Ch. 3) played on the higher strings and uses string bends (*Basics 1*: Ch. 7).

The bridge [C] features a pumping harder rock figure based on a open low E and the octave above. Play the open 6th string and E on the 5th string/7th fret together as a two-note "chord" or diad (*Basics 1*: p. 58). This is a great part to help you get a feel for a steady eighth-note groove. (Refer to *Basics 1*: p. 19 for more on eighth notes.)

The chorus [D] exploits a secondary riff. This one is in C and is a movable riff (see *Basics 2*).

The ensemble lick in bars 63-66 should present no problems once you learn the pentatonic box concepts covered in *Basics 2* and *3*.

From the Capitol recording THE BEATLES (WHITE ALBUM)

Birthday

Words and Music by John Lennon and Paul McCartney

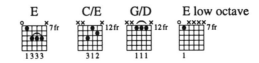

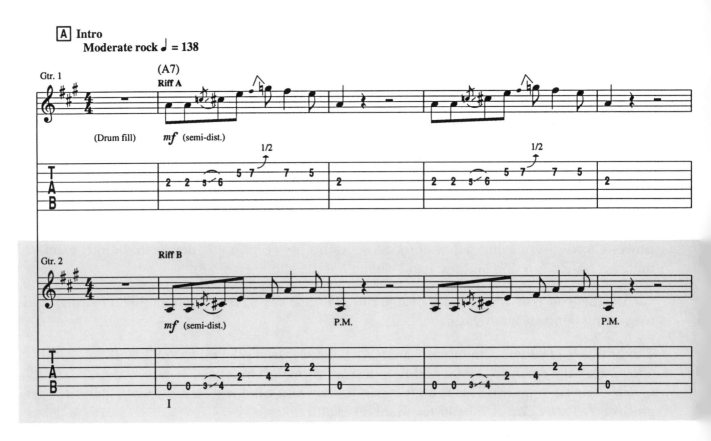

MCA music publishing

B 1st Verse

Gtr. 1: w/ Riff A
Gtr. 2

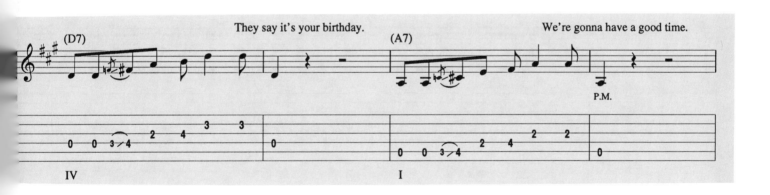

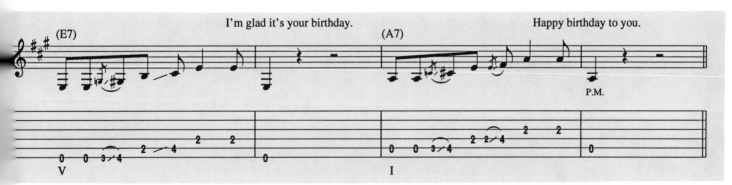

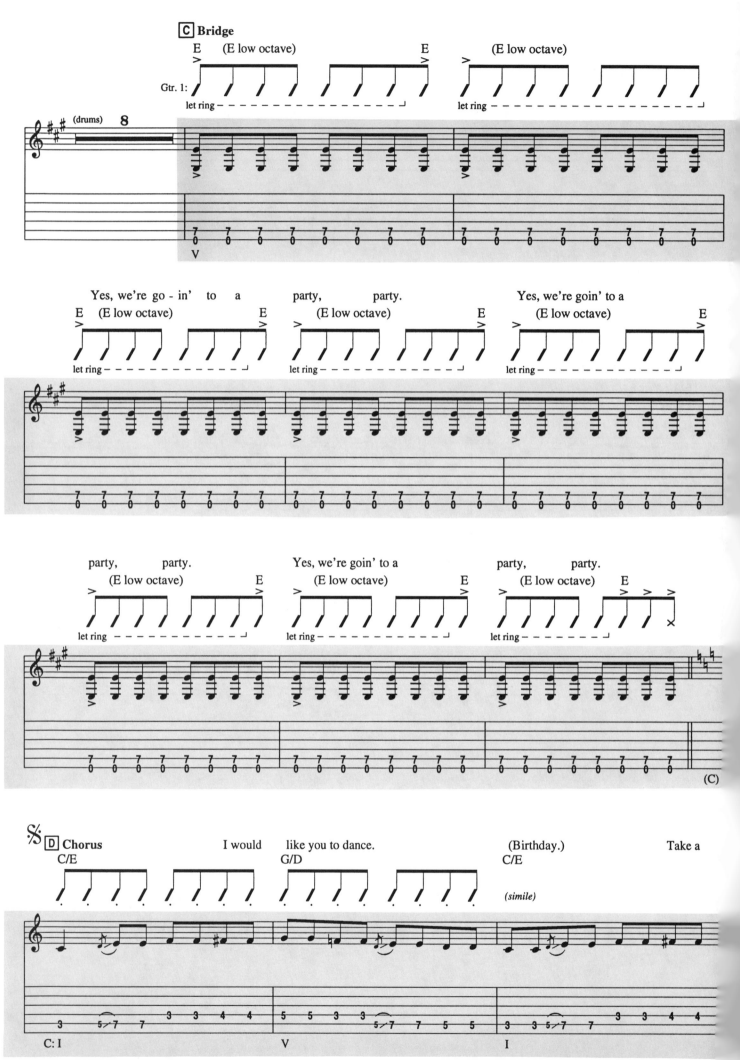

ch - ch - ch - chance.　　　　　(Birthday.)　　　　　I would　like you to dance.

(Birthday.)　　　　Dance! _____　Yeah!

(2nd time) To Coda ⊕

Gtr. 1: w/Fill 1, 1st time
Gtr. 1: w/Fill 2, 2nd time
Gtr. 2: tacet 2nd time

N.C.

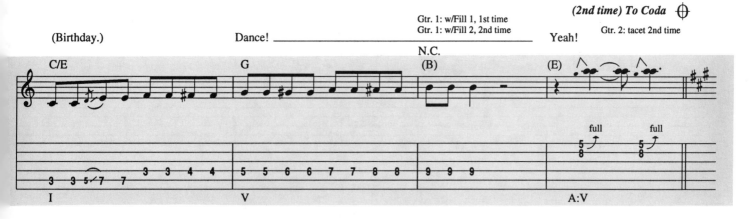

E **Interlude**

Gtr. 1: w/Riff A
Gtr. 2　　　(A7)

Fill 1
Gtr. 1

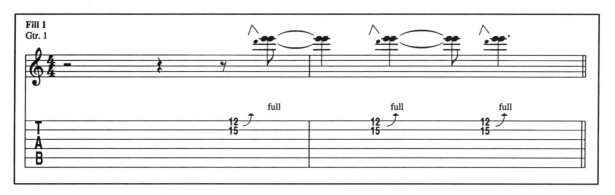

Fill 2
Gtr. 1

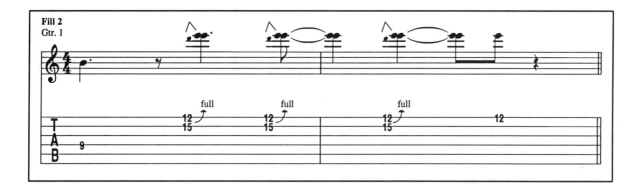

9

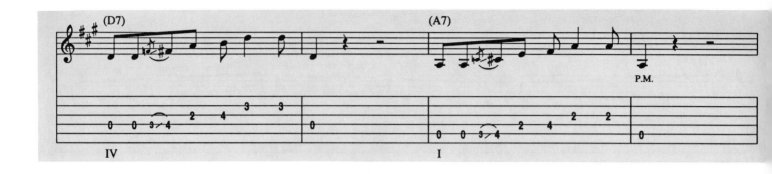

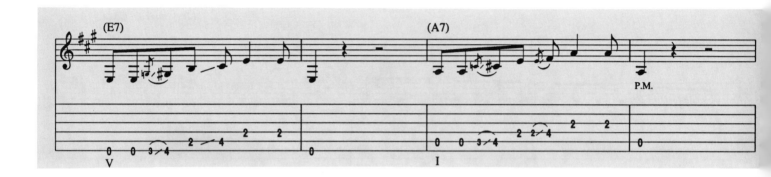

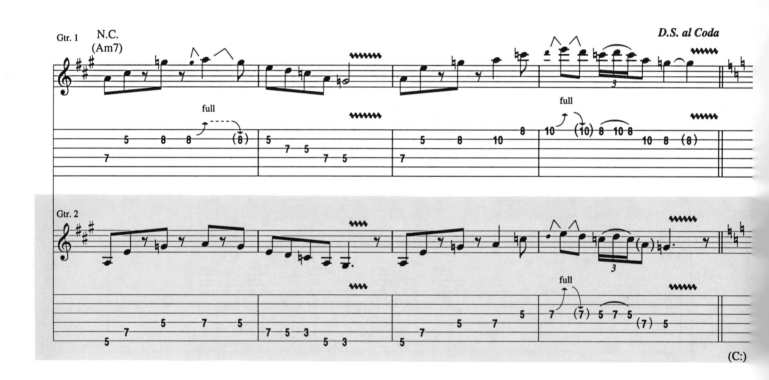

⊕ *Coda*

F 2nd Verse

Gtr. 1: w/Riff A, 1st 8 bars only
Gtr. 2

I'm glad it's your birthday.   Happy

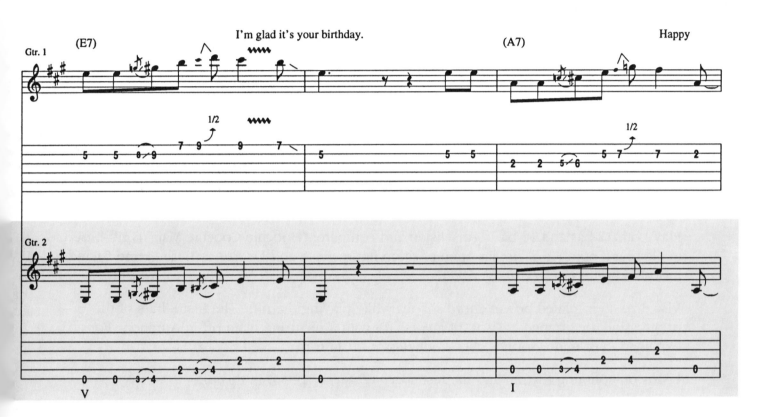

birthday to you.

* Flick pickup selector switch to change tone while sustaining final note.

I'M YOUR HOOCHIE COOCHIE MAN
Muddy Waters

An immortal Chicago Blues standard written by the great Willie Dixon, this song is a perennial favorite covered and recorded by countless artists including Jimi Hendrix and Johnny Winter. The definitive version belongs to Muddy Waters who recorded it in 1953.

This is an ideal piece for exploring the slow blues shuffle in 12/8 meter. (See *Basics 1*: pp. 39-42.)

Notice the slightly altered (enlarged) blues form of the song. It follows a 16-bar structure in A as opposed to the typical 12-bar structure of most blues songs. Nonetheless the I, IV and V chord changes and their order remain true to standard blues form. (For more on the 12-bar progression and blues form refer to *Basics 1*: Ch. 4.)

Play both 12-bar and 16-bar forms, listen and compare. "Hoochie Coochie Man" is riff-based, exploiting a number of similar open position figures in A and D (*Basics 1*: Ch. 3 and 5) and a movable figure in E (*Basics 2*: Ch. 3).

Visualize their related power chord shapes while playing the riffs. The first 8 bars of the progression are arranged as sort of a verse [B] with a recurring main riff in A minor. (For an explanation of minor sounds check out *Basics 1*: Ch. 6.)

Focus on counting rhythm and the rest space (*Basics 2*: p. 43) in this riff.

The verse's minor sound contrasts nicely with the dominant seventh sound of the riffs in the choruses [C], [D] and [E] (*Basics 3*: p. 31).

The turnaround figures in bars 17 and 25 are a perfect example of the triplet blues riff (*Basics 1*: p. 41) in action.

I'm Your Hoochie Coochie Man

Words and Music by Willie Dixon

BOPPIN' THE BLUES
Carl Perkins

Carl Perkins is one of the founding fathers of the rockabilly guitar style and therefore rightfully a godfather of the entire rock genre. His unique country/swing/rock/blues approach was highly influential, affecting the work of important subsequent players like George Harrison, James Burton and Brian Setzer among many others. "Boppin' The Blues" was his second single, a followup to his hit "Blue Suede Shoes", and captures many of the trademark elements that make rockabilly such an exciting and vital music and Carl such a conspicuous proponent.

The verses and choruses are full of boogie-woogie-inspired, bass-line type riffs in open position. (Refer to *Basics 1*: Ch. 5.) These are played with both conventional flat picking and Carl's pick-and-finger hybrid picking style (*Basics 2*: p. 57).

Be sure to visualize the open power chord shapes of A5, D5 and E5 as you finger these riffs. They are played essentially in quarter-note and eighth-note rhythm (*Basics 1*: Ch. 1 and 2) with the distinct swing of an early rock and roll shuffle groove.

Note the X's throughout the guitar part. This is a study in fret-hand muting (*Basics 1*: p. 22) as a musical effect. Additionally, every time you see a staccato dot below or above a note head (*Basics 2*: p. 62) play it short by releasing your fret-hand pressure just after striking the note.

The form is a 12-bar blues progression in A (*Basics 1*: Ch. 4 and 5) with slight internal variations in the choruses [C], [E] and [G]. Here the IV chord, D, gets held one bar longer than normally expected. (See bar 31.)

The guitar solo [F] is simple but effective and predominantly chord-based using movable ninth and seventh shapes and triads (*Basics 2*: p. 47 and *Advanced Concepts*), movable three-note power chords (*Basics 2*: p. 20) and an open A5 shape (*Basics 1*: Ch. 2) at the close.

The tag [K] presents a western swing-oriented cadence phrase which is a cliche of the country and rockabilly style. The chords in this section are a bit more difficult to master than open power chords or simple riffs but well worth the effort.

Boppin' The Blues

Words and Music by Howard Griffin and Carl Perkins

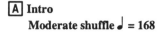

Moderate shuffle ♩ = 168

Well, all my friends are boppin' the blues; it must be goin' 'round.

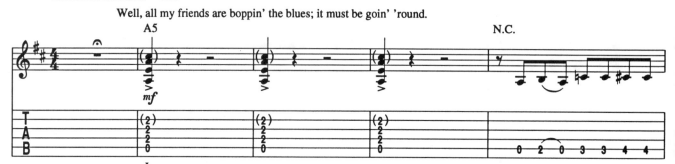

All my friends are boppin' the blues; it must be goin' around. I love you, baby, but

I must be rhythm bound. 1. Well, the doctor told me

"Carl, you don't need no pills." Hey, the doctor told me, "Boy, you don't need no

pills. Just a handful a' nickels, a juke - box'll cure your ills."

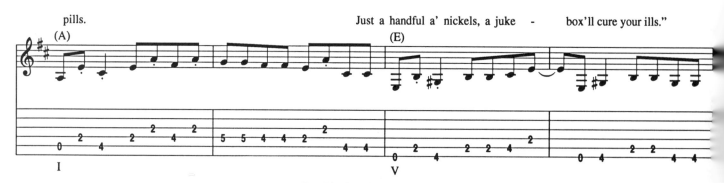

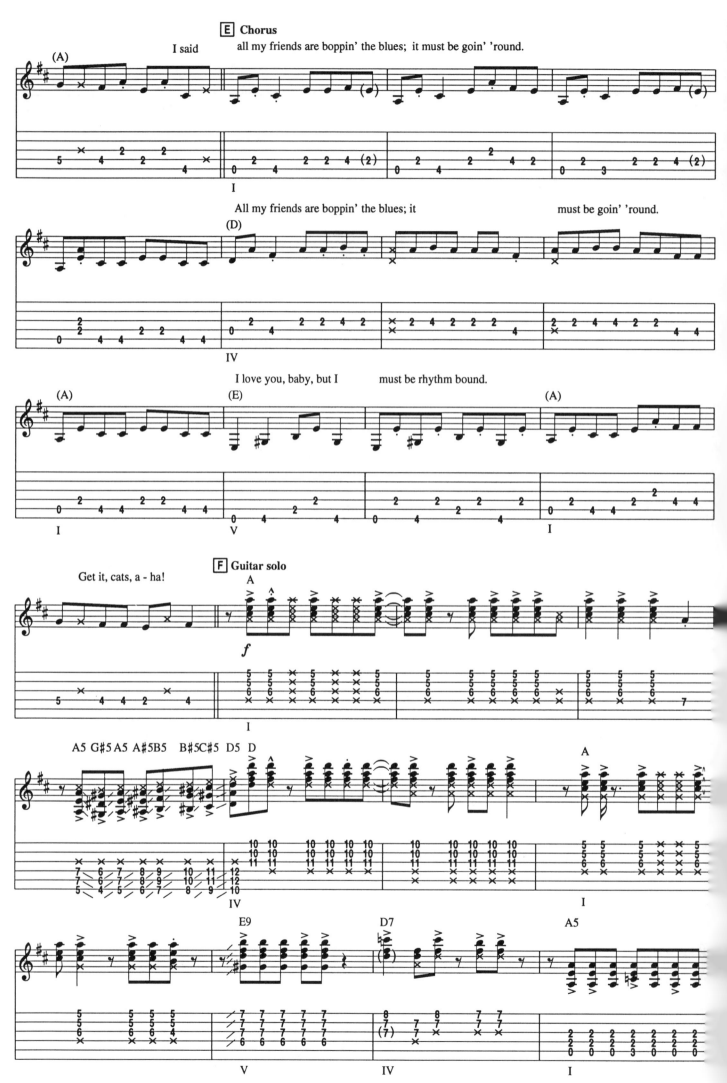

I CAN SEE FOR MILES
The Who

This mid-Sixties British Invasion classic set the stage for hard rock and metal with its extreme volume, heavy accents and sheer bombast.

The opening chord riff and its variants throughout the song are based on a simple open E5 chord (*Basics 1*: Ch. 2) and related open G5 and A5 shapes. (These are barred as shown in *Basics 1*: p. 16.)

The progression heard during the intro [A], verses [B], [D], [F], [I] and the interlude [H]: E—G—A, introduces an unconventional chord relationship common to rock, metal and pop music. Here the G major chord in the key of E or III chord is found. This is outside the key center and therein lies its impact and charm. (For a brief explanation of key centers see *Basics 1*: p. 34.)

In the choruses, a unison interval [C] (*Basics 1*: last photo) and open string unison bends [C], [E], [G] (*Basics 1*: Ch. 7) are used structurally as riffs.

In the outchorus [L], higher unison bends (*Basics 2*: p. 36) continue the idea.

Notice the backing progression in the choruses. Besides the I, IV and V chords you also find G [III], C (the VI chord), and D (the VII chord). These are two other standard rock changes and come from the use of modal harmony (explained and covered in *Advanced Concepts*).

In the interlude [H] Pete Townsend gives us a serious workout on alternate-picked sixteenth notes (*Basics 1*: p. 28). Be aware of the accents and the pull-offs and hammer-ons (*Basics 3*) in this section.

From the MCA recording MEATY, BEATY, BIG AND BOUNCY

I Can See For Miles

Words and Music by Peter Townshend

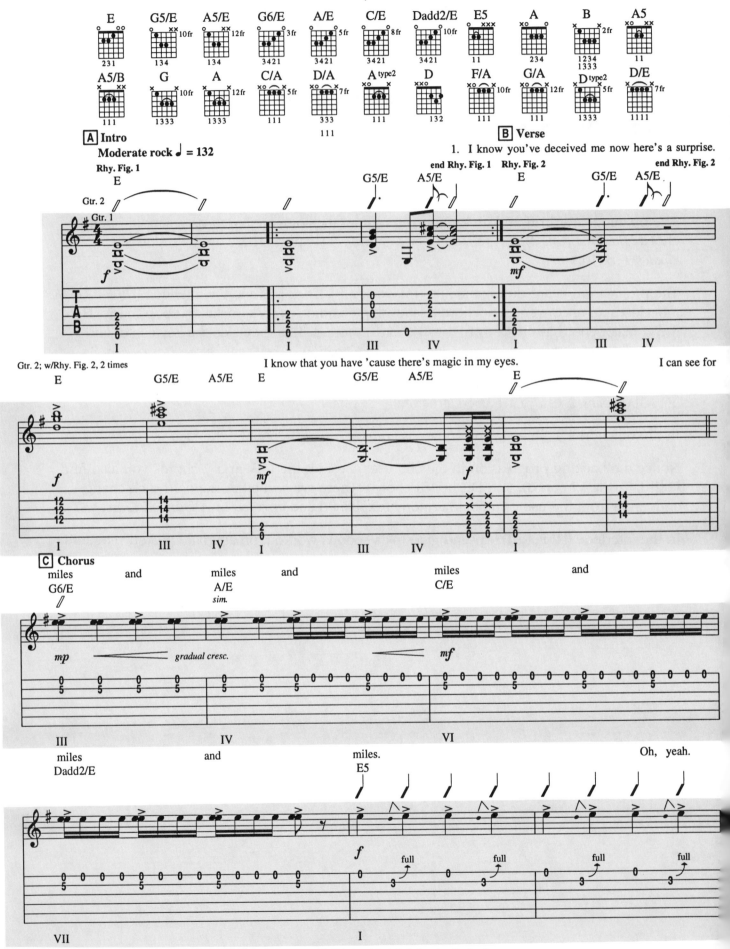

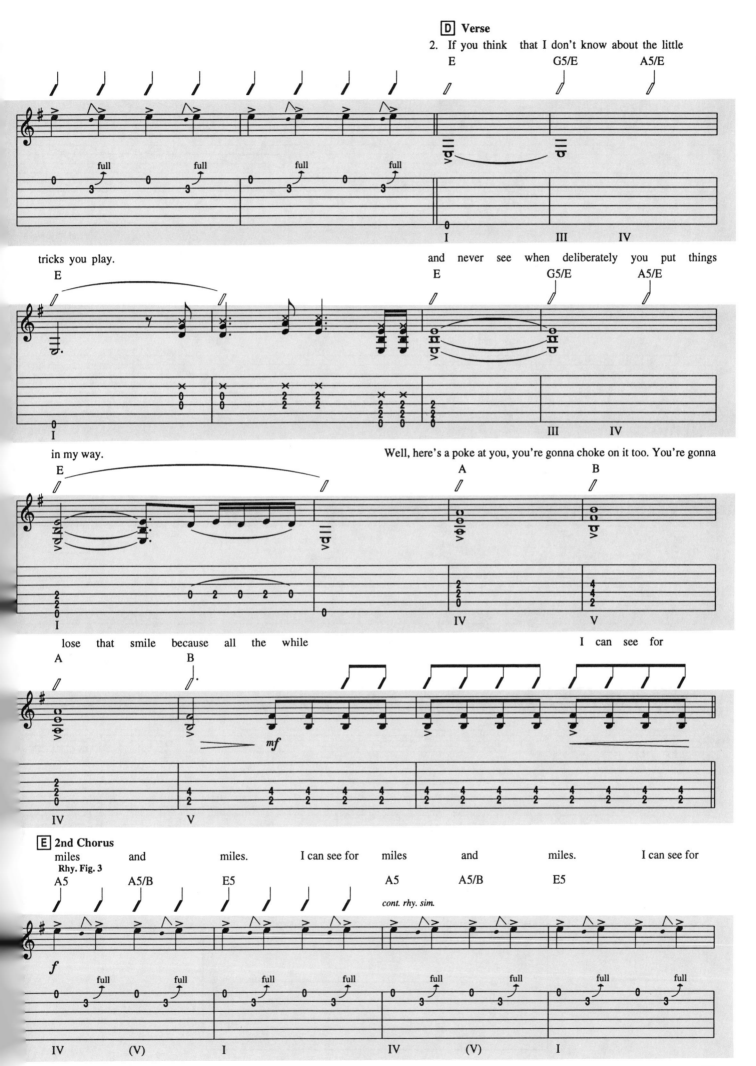

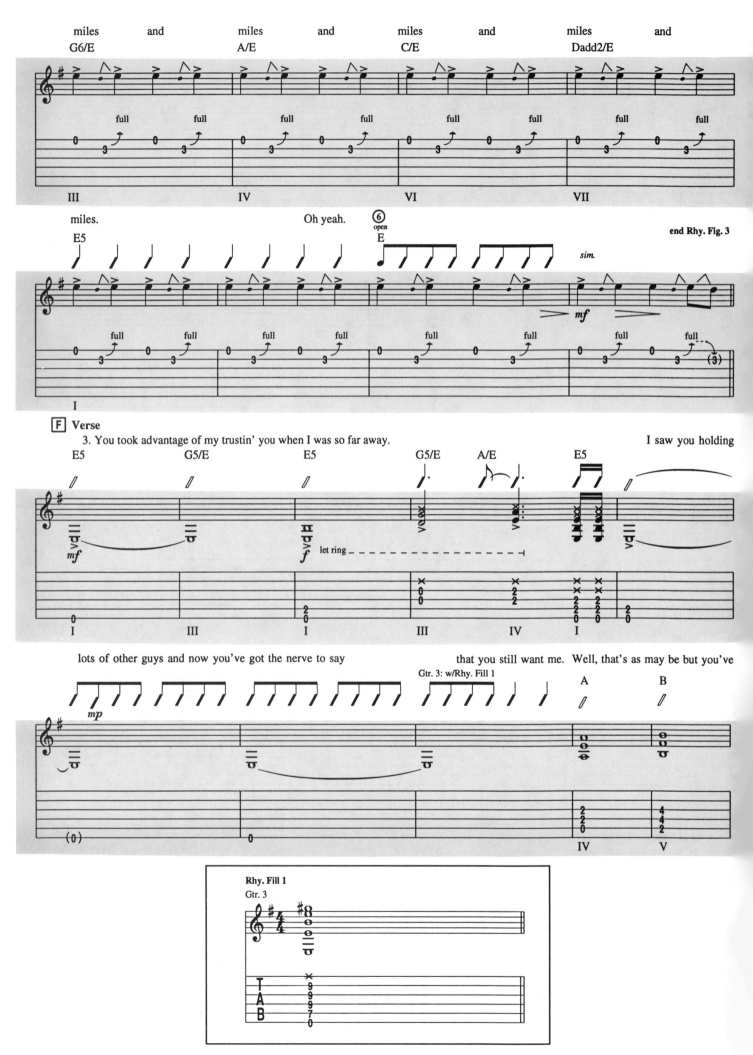

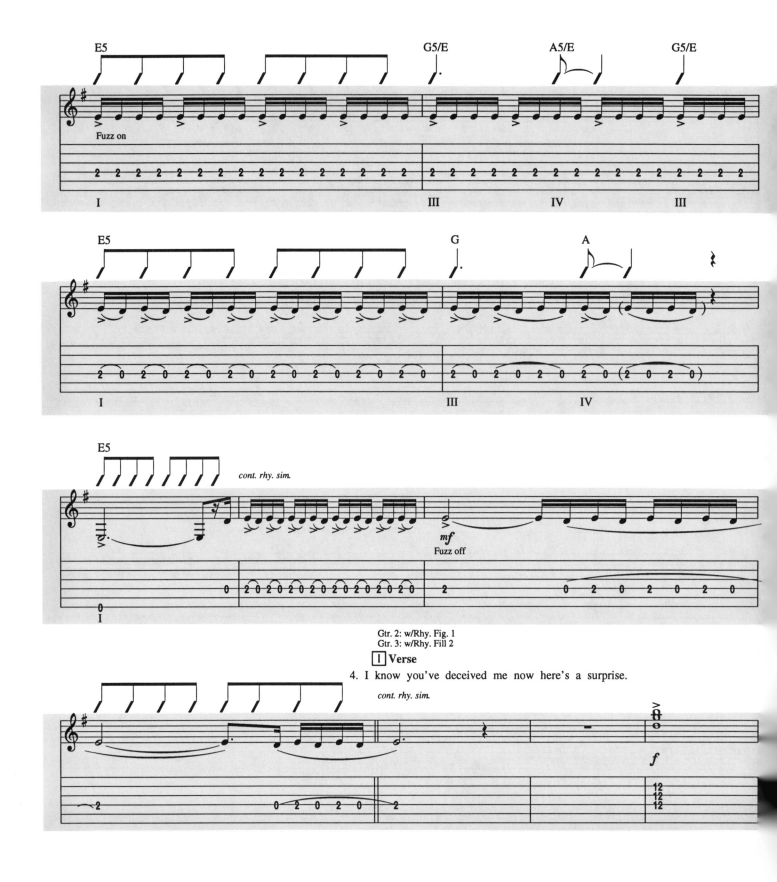

Gtr. 2: w/Rhy. Fig. 1
Gtr. 3: w/Rhy. Fill 2

I Verse

4. I know you've deceived me now here's a surprise.

cont. rhy. sim.

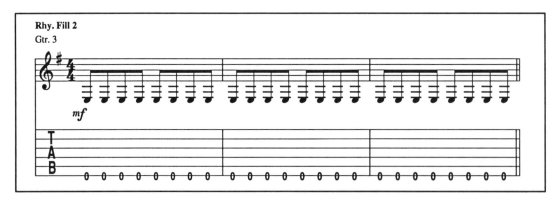

Rhy. Fill 2
Gtr. 3

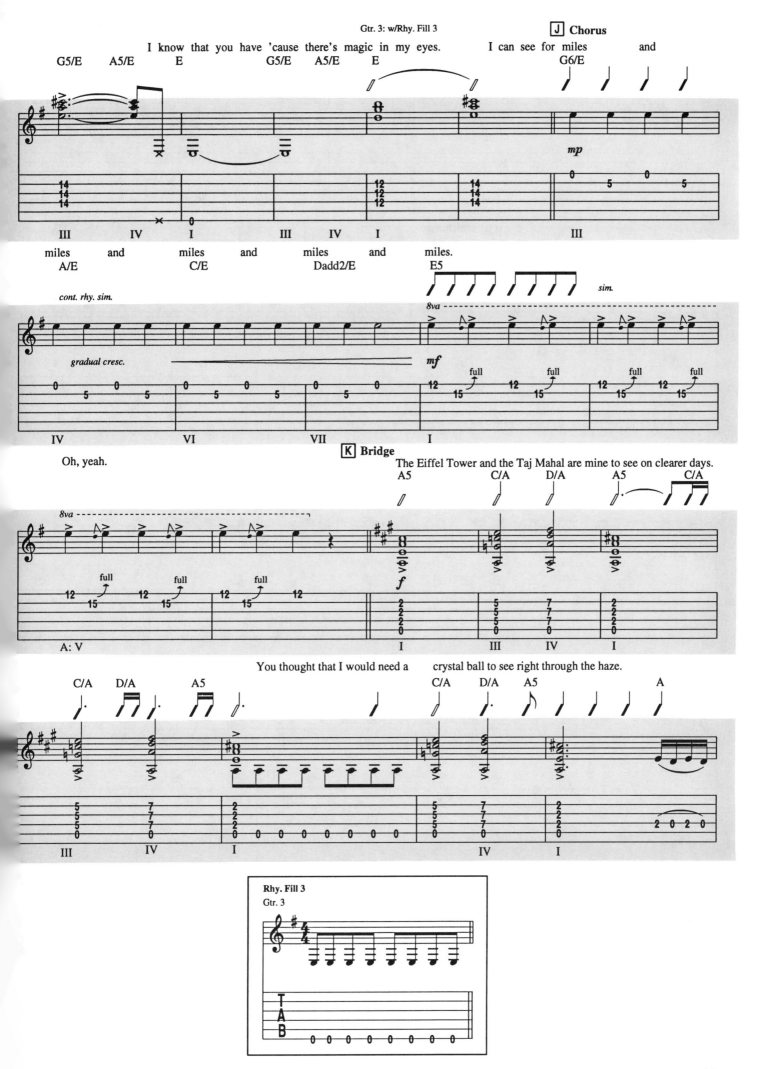

Well, here's a poke at you, you're gonna choke on it too. You're gonna lose that smile because all the while

L Outchorus

I can see for miles and miles. I can see for miles and

miles. I can see for miles and miles and miles and miles and

miles and miles and miles and miles.

I can see for miles and miles. I can see for

Repeat and fade out

SWEET EMOTION
Aerosmith

An all-time classic hard rock tune, and one of the finest in the Aerosmith catalog, "Sweet Emotion" is a model of riff-based composition. You can think of all the riffs as being in A (or on A).

Riffs A and B found in the verses [B] and [C] are exemplary. These are simple but powerful figures based on the underlying open A5 power chord shape (*Basics 1*: Ch. 1 and 2).

The chord change of D to A in Riff B (basically the main riff) establishes a IV to I sound in the key of A (*Basics 1*: p. 34).

Both guitars play the aggressive ensemble figure at bars 17 and 29. They begin in unison and end up in parallel fifth harmony two bars later. This means they are playing the same melody a fifth apart. (Check out the interval chart in *Basics 1*: p. 11 for reference as well as the interval music builder in *Basics 1* on page 58.)

The chorus [D] has its own secondary riff. This one is also based on the open A5 power chord shape. As with Riffs A and B, visualize the A5 chord shape as you play the figure.

The chorus riff incorporates a couple of pull-offs and hammer-ons (*Basics 3*) which may seem tricky at first but will feel very natural and fluid with a little practice and familiarity.

Sweet Emotion

Words and Music by Steven Tyler and Tom Hamilton

C Verse

2. Some sweet talkin' mama with a face like a gent,
4. You stand in front just a shakin' yo' ass.

said my
I'll take

get up and go must've got up and went.
you backstage; you can drink from my glass.

Well, I
I'm

got good news, she's a real good liar,
talkin' 'bout somethin' you can sure understand.

'cause my   backstage boogie, set yo' pants on fire.
'cause a   month on the road and I'll be eatin' from your hand.

RAMBLIN' ON MY MIND
Blues Breakers – John Mayall
with Eric Clapton

In 1966, Eric Clapton rewrote the rule book on electric blues guitar and influenced generations of modern bluesmen and hard rock players to follow with his work on John Mayall's *Blues Breakers* album. Amidst the burning numbers like "Have You Heard", "Hideaway", "Key To Love" and "Steppin' Out", he felt inclined to step out and debut as lead vocalist on this subdued, atmospheric blues piece.

A sultry Robert Johnson composition, "Ramblin" is a perfect example of a slow blues shuffle in 12/8 time. (See *Basics 1*: pp. 39-42.) It also contains some very definitive open position blues comping (*Basics 1*: Ch. 4) in E throughout.

The accompaniment in the verses [B] follows the E5–E6–E7–E6, I chord, pattern consistently and transfers virtually the same exact pattern to A for the IV chord. These can be seen in essence as the same comping figure moved to different roots and based on the open E5 and A5 power chords (*Basics 1*: Ch. 1 and 2).

The trills found in the third bar of the intro [A] and verse [B] are similarly based on an open chord shape. Visualize them as part of the open E7 shape. (See *Basics 2*: p. 59.)

The form of the piece is a traditional 12-bar blues progression with a IV chord in the second measure. (See *Basics 1*: Ch. 4 and *Basics 2*: pp. 8-13 for more information.) The open B7, V chord (introduced in *Basics 2*: p. 61) is easy to finger even for beginners and adds a nice appropriately rustic touch to the intro in bar 4 and the verse comping in bar 13.

Note that Clapton varies his picking during the song alternating between normal flat picked and hybrid picked approaches in the verses.

The guitar solo [C] is soulful and simple based largely on string bending ostinato riffs. (Refer to *Basics 1*: p. 62.) This is a moderately challenging solo for the beginning to intermediate player on a technical level and should present no problems for the guitarist who works on the lead guitar licks in *Basics 1* and *Basics 2*. (The major pentatonic box in bars 25-29 is thoroughly explored early in *Basics 3*.)

Throughout the piece you'll find parallel sixths in turnarounds—for example, in bars 3, 19, 31 and 33. Compare these shapes to the diad depicted in Fig. 41 in *Basics 2*: Ch. 5. This is their chord of origin. A great deal of blues, rock and roll and country guitar playing utilizes this humble two-note voicing.

In the coda, bar 34, two new chords are heard: D#7 and E7. These share the same shape and derive their basic form from the open D7 voicing in *Basics 2*: p. 60. Just fret the the root on the 4th string, refinger using all four fingers and you have the movable version heard in the last bar of "Ramblin' On My Mind".

Ramblin' On My Mind

Words and Music by Robert Johnson

I've __ got
I'm go - in'
Lit - tle

ram - blin', _____
down to the sta - tion, __
girl, lit - tle girl, _____

w/Fill 2, 2nd time
w/Fill 4, 3rd time

I've got ram - blin' all on my mind. _____
catch that old fast milk - train, __ you'll see. _____
I've got mean things all on my mind. _____

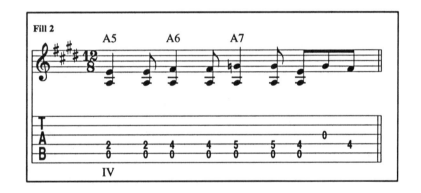

Fill 2

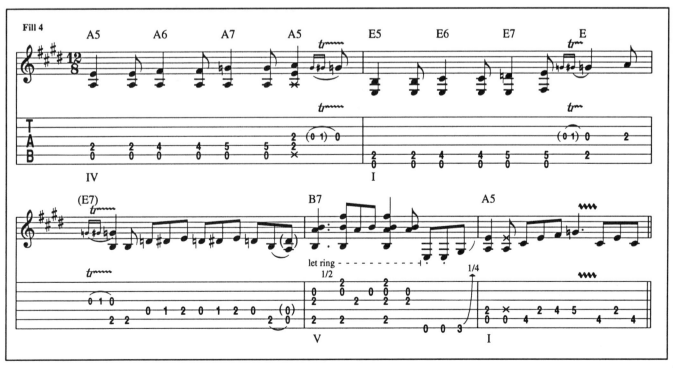

Fill 4

35

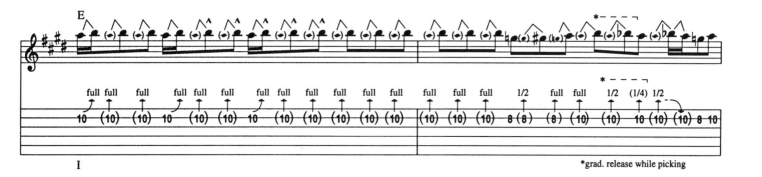

*grad. release while picking

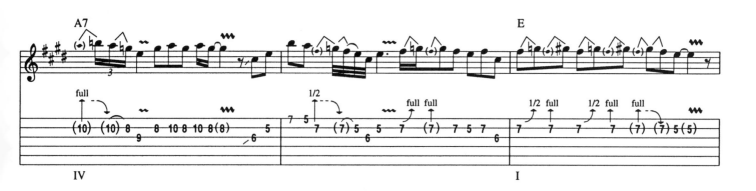

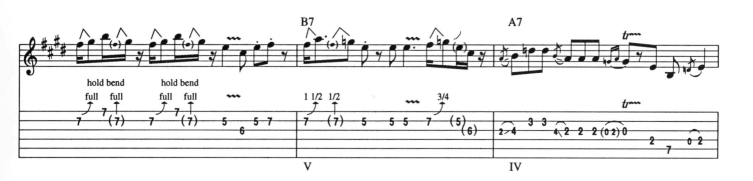

D.S.(3rd verse) al Coda
(take 1st ending)

3. I got

*vibrato all notes slightly.

BANG A GONG (GET IT ON)
T. Rex

This early-Seventies offering from Marc Bolan and T.Rex is considered to be one of the all-time classic rock tunes of the era. Power Station attested to its longevity when they covered it in the mid-Eighties. It is an ideal song to study for simplicity and groove.

The main riff is heard throughout the piece—in the intro, the verses, the choruses and the outro. Played by Gtr. 1, it uses the fifth-to-sixth comping figure introduced in *Basics 1* on pages 37 and 38. This figure is played in E and in A in the verses.

Visualize the open E5 and A5 power chord shapes as you work on the riff. There is an interesting twist to the riff. Though it is arranged in straight eighth-note rhythm, the accenting on the upbeats: "three-**and**, four-**and**" gives it an odd emphasis which is known as syncopation.

What is syncopation? Syncopation is a rhythmical device commonly found in rock, jazz, R&B, pop and many other forms of music. It is created by emphasizing weak beats or weak parts of beats instead of strong beats. This is generally done by tying over strong beats (duration), replacing them with a rest (space) or accenting them, as in this case. Practice counting and stressing these parts of the beat by repeating this figure: "**ONE**-and, *two*-and, three-**and**, four-**and**".

The fills played by Gtr. 2 (bar 5 and 6) are a secondary riff also heard consistently through the song. These are simple diads (*Basics 1*: p. 58) on the open first and second strings. They are struck in a recurring Morse Code-type pattern to produce the riff which is more rhythmic than melodic.

In the memorable anthem-like chorus [D], a G major chord is found in the progression. This would be the III chord of the key of E. (See "I Can See For Miles" and also refer to the chart in *Basics 1* on page 34 for more on chord numerals.) This chord change is a staple of rock harmony heard in such tunes as "Purple Haze", "I'm Not Your Stepping Stone" and "For Your Love".

Gtr. 1's part in the chorus relies on quarter-note rhythm while Gtr. 2 plays steady eighth notes in this section.

The outro [F] contains a brief E minor pentatonic lick which is played in the most common pentatonic box shape in the 12th position. (See *Basics 1*: p. 32 for more on positions.) Realize that this is the octave-higher version of the pentatonic scale shapes shown in *Basics 1*: Ch. 6.

Similarly, the string bends on the G string are also octave-higher versions of the ideas presented in *Basics 1*: Ch. 7 and thoroughly explored in *Basics 2*: Ch. 4. For now try to slowly and carefully master this simple lead line even though it may seem a bit out of your immediate reach. This is a very accessible lick for beginning to intermediate guitarists and with just a little extra effort you will find it quite playable.

From the Reprise recording ELECTRIC WARRIOR

Bang A Gong (Get It On)

Words and Music by Marc Bolan

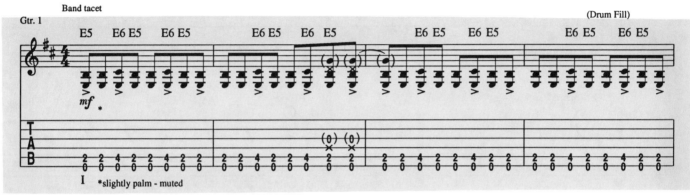

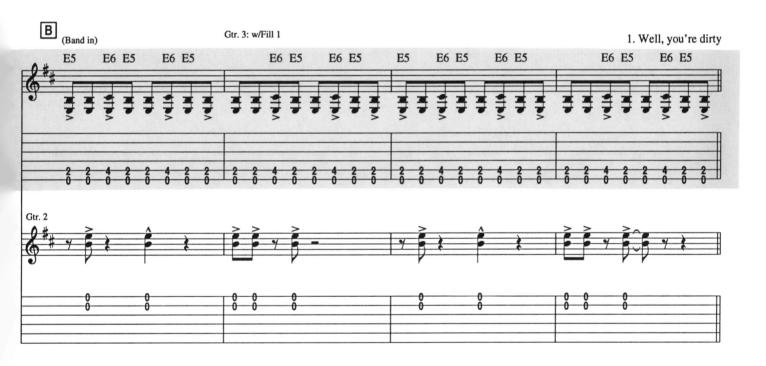

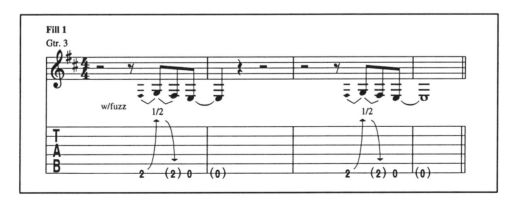

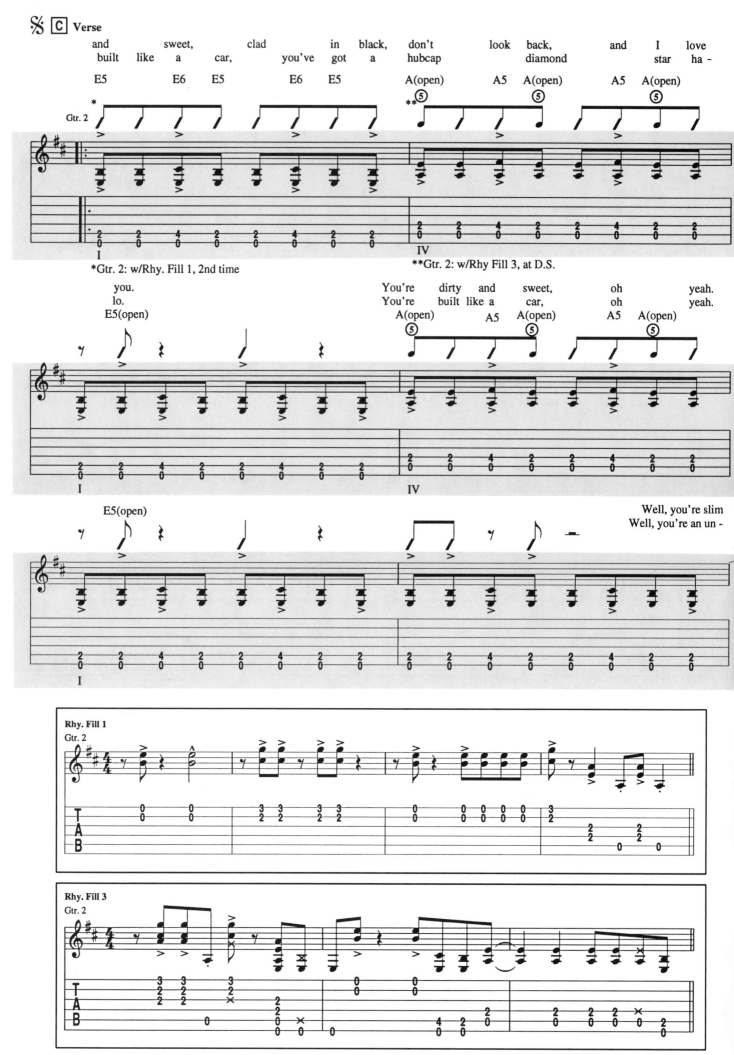

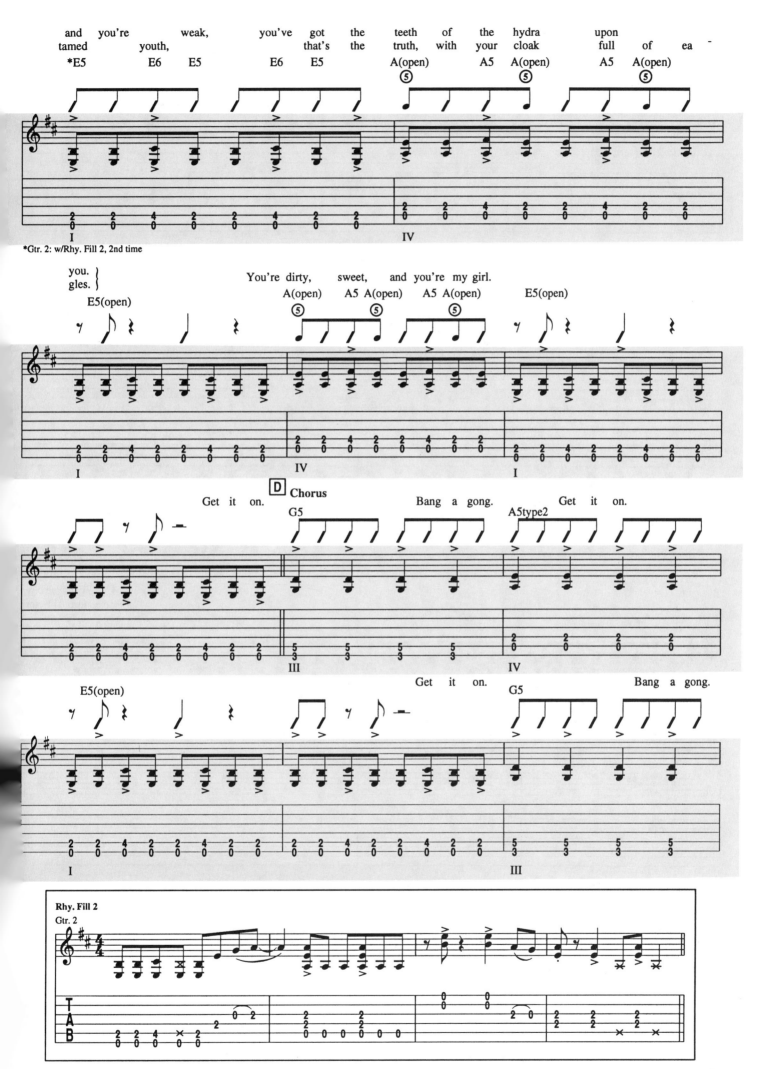

*Gtr. 2: w/Rhy. Fill 2, 2nd time

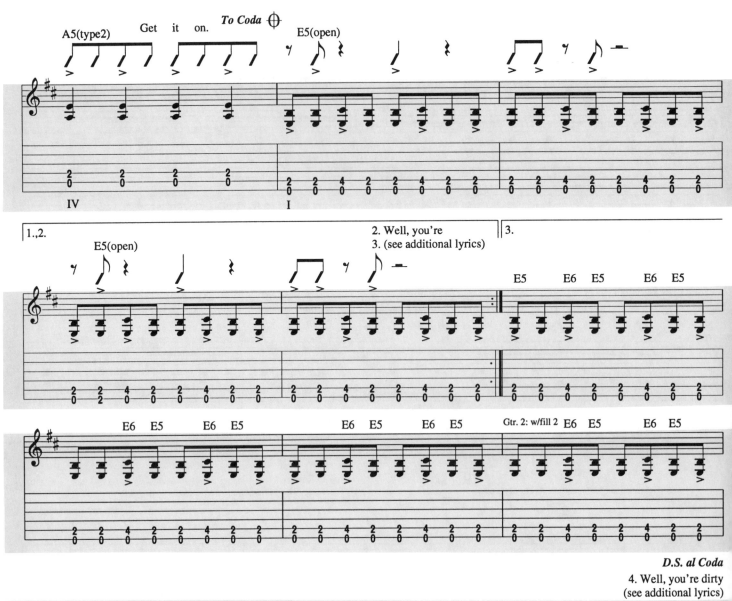

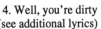

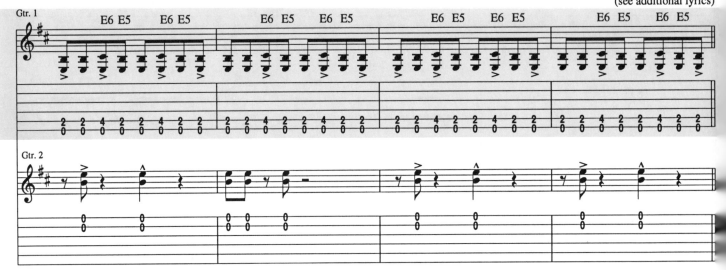

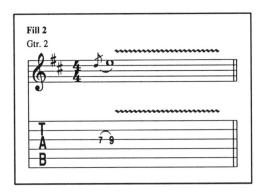

⊕ *Coda*

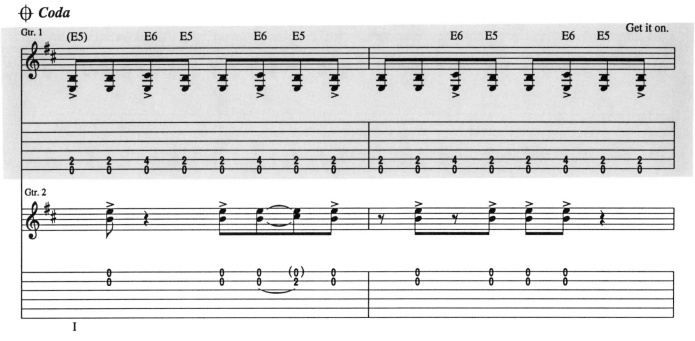

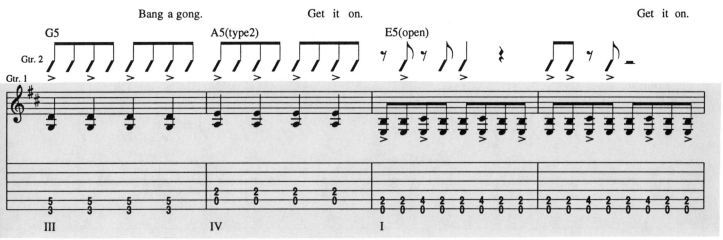

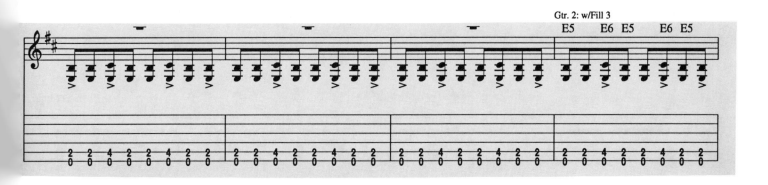

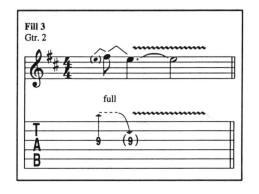

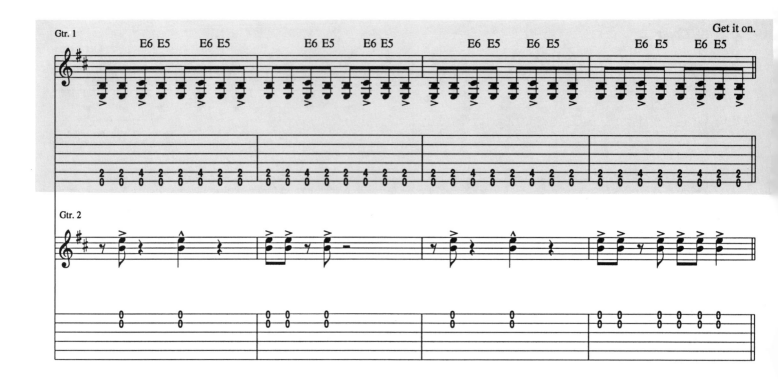

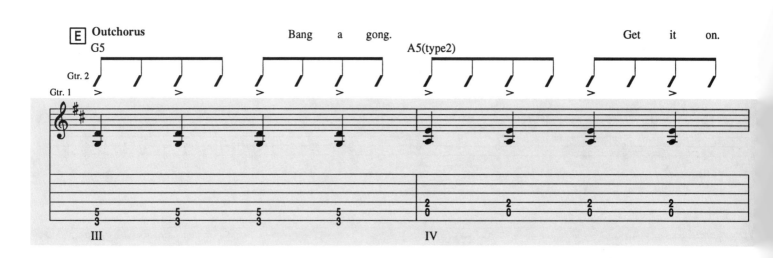

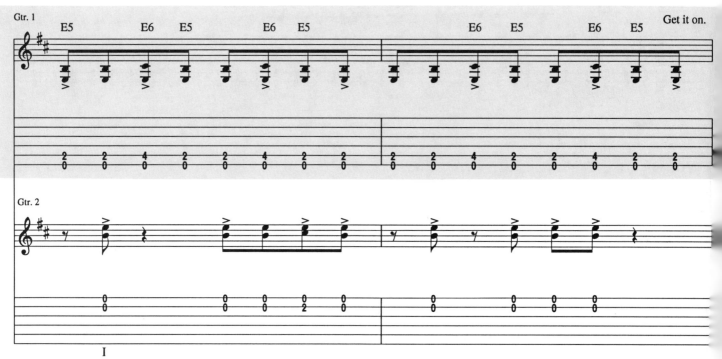

44

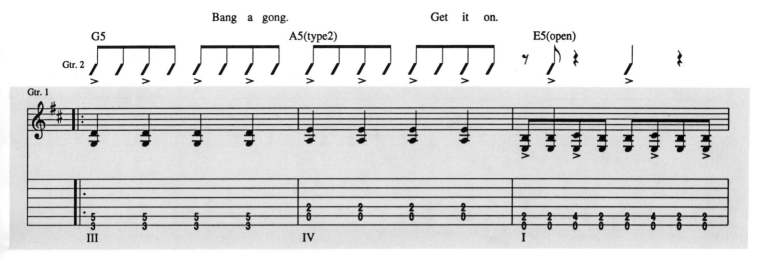

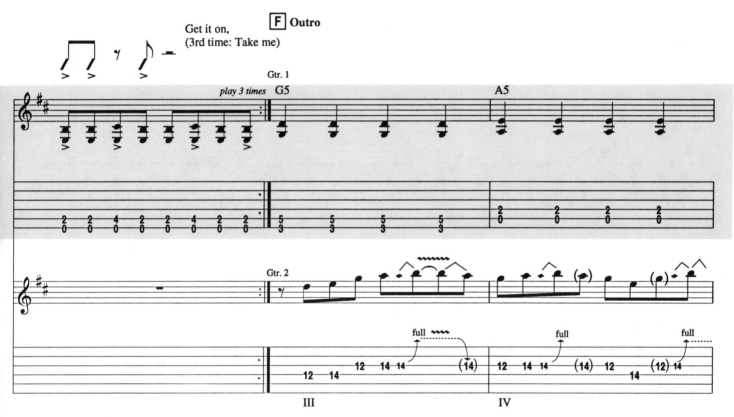

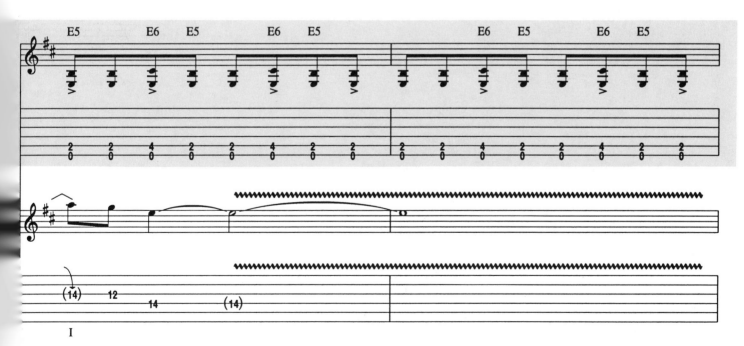

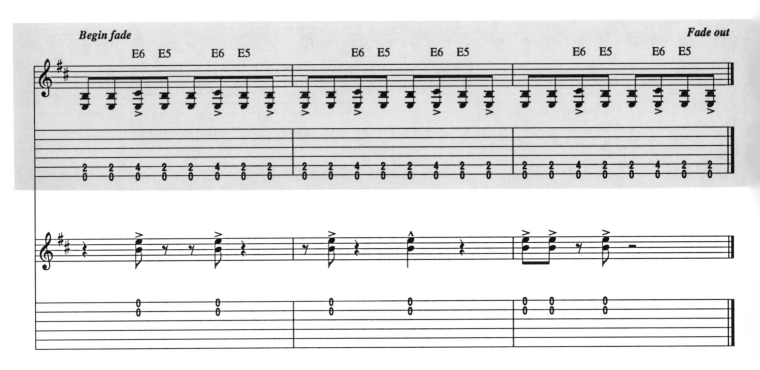

Additional Lyrics

Verse 3:
Well, you're windy and wild,
You've got the blues in your shoes
And you're stockings.
You're windy and wild, oh yeah.
Well, you're built like a car.
You've got a hubcap diamond star halo.
You're dirty, sweet and you're my girl.
(To Chorus:)

Verse 4:
Well, you're dirty and sweet,
Clad in black, don't look back and I love you.
You're dirty and sweet, oh yeah.
You dance when you walk
So let's dance, take a chance, understand me.
You're dirty, sweet and you're my girl.
(To Chorus:)

GET BACK
The Beatles

The Beatles got back to their rock and roll roots in this gutsy song from their 1969 movie, *Let It Be*. Eschewing their customary studio wizardry, they opted for a no-frills live recording approach and an edgy, first-take type of performance. John Lennon played lead guitar on this song with George Harrison accompanying on rhythm guitar—another change in their usual m.o.

Let's focus on George's playing, written as Gtr. 2. His almost spartan simplicity and straightforward rhythm makes the part eminently suitable for our purposes. This is a great part for learning to count and feel basic eighth notes, quarter notes and the common "one-and, two-*and*" syncopation. (See explanation of syncopation in "Bang A Gong".)

The intro [A] figure gets things rolling with a steady eighth-note groove built on the open A5 power chord shape (*Basics 1*: Ch. 2) and two heavily accented attacks on open G and D chords (*Basics 2*: Ch. 5). You'll find this progression is a familiar one in rock, heard in the music of AC/DC, Van Halen and countless other bands.

Notice the fret-hand muting (*Basics 1*: p. 22) and alternating A5 diad approach used in the first three bars. George maintains this approach throughout the verses [B] but adds an open D5 chord (*Basics 1*: p. 18) for the I to IV (A5–D5) change in the rhythm part.

At the chorus [C] fret-hand muting becomes an important element of the figure in bars 14 and 15 and particularly behind the guitar solo at [D].

John's rhythm part (Gtr. 1) makes use of movable blues comping (see *Basics 2*: pp. 11-13) in the intro and verse sections as well as behind the piano solo and in the tag.

In the choruses, he plays a movable riff (*Basics 2*: Ch. 3) and high seventh-chord pattern that has a Motown-inspired R&B feel. The seventh chord takes its shape from the open D7 form introduced in *Basics 2* on page 60.

Additionally, John takes two funky guitar solos at [D] and [G]. These are based on major and minor pentatonic boxes and string bending concepts found in *Basics 2* and *Basics 3*.

Get Back

Words and Music by John Lennon and Paul McCartney

MCA music publishing

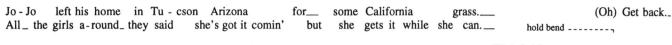

Jo - Jo   left his home in Tu - cson Arizona   for__ some California   grass.__   (Oh) Get back..

All_ the girls a-round_ they said   she's got it comin'   but   she gets it while she can. __

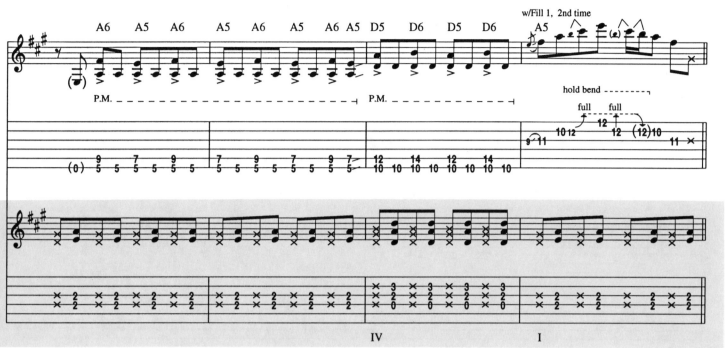

C **Chorus**

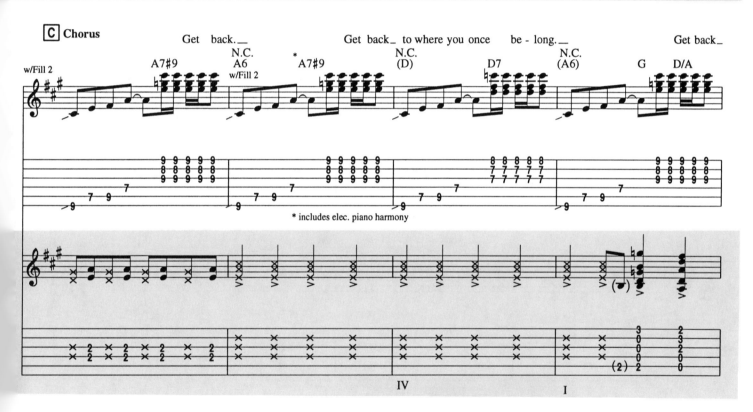

* includes elec. piano harmony

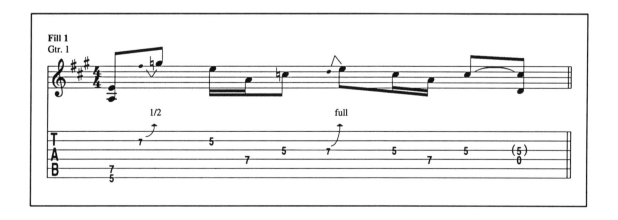

Fill 1
Gtr. 1

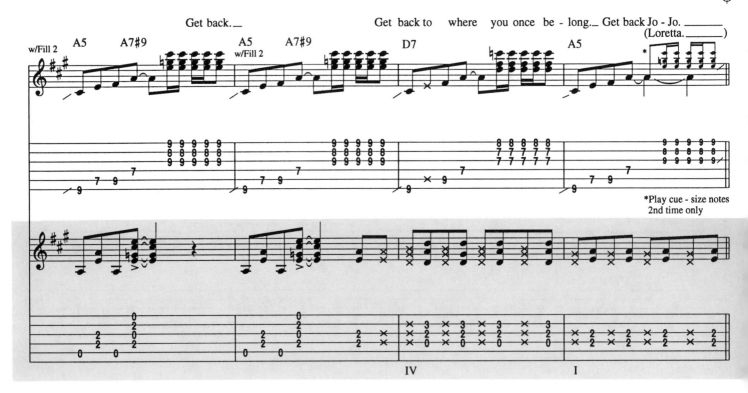

Get back. __   Get back to   where   you once be - long. __ Get back Jo - Jo. _____
(Loretta. _____)

*Play cue - size notes
2nd time only

D **1st Guitar Solo**

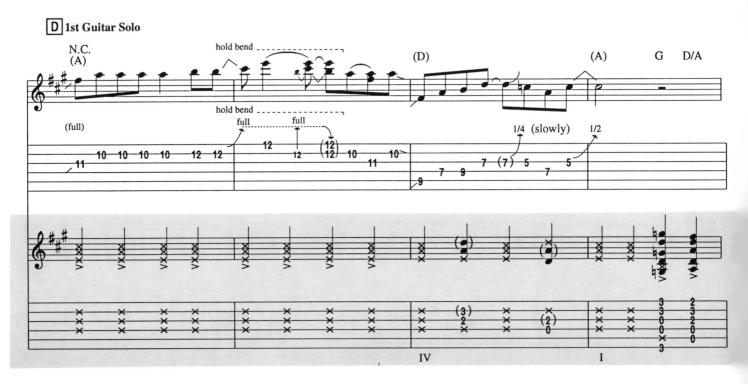

Fill 2
Gtr. 3 (elec. piano arr. for guitar)

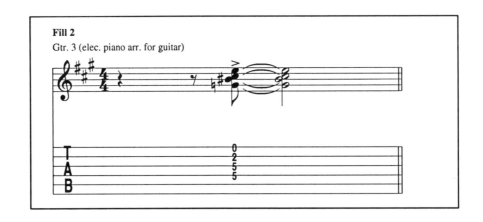

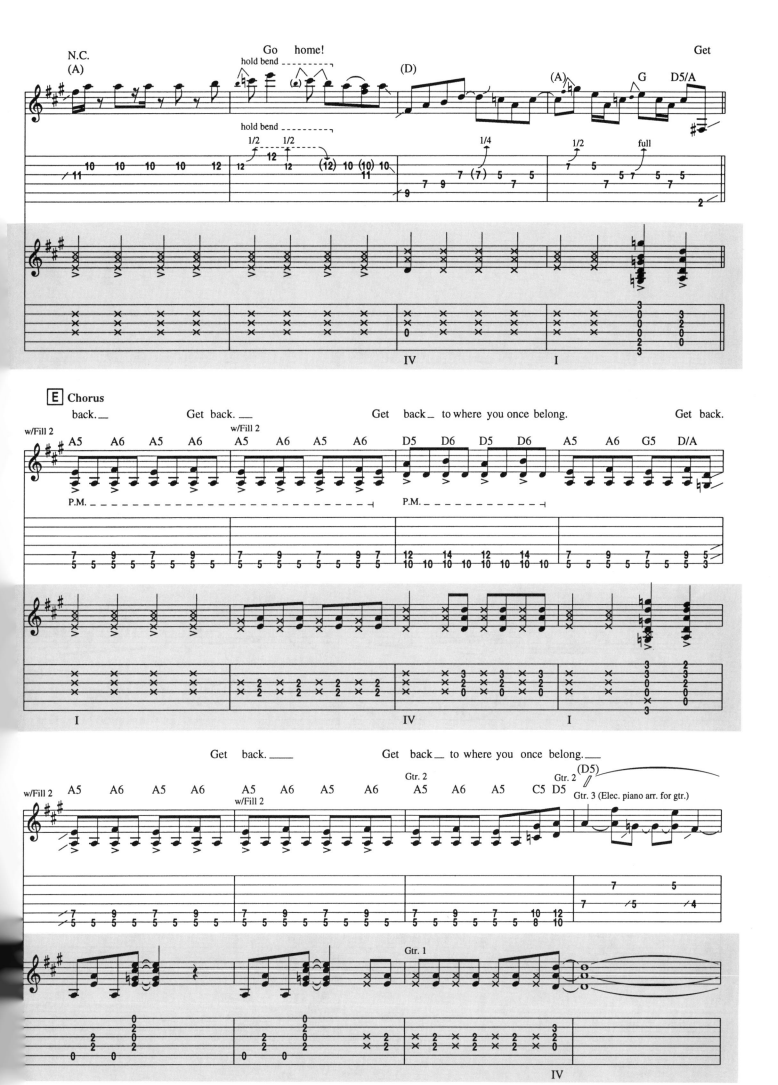

Get back, Jo!

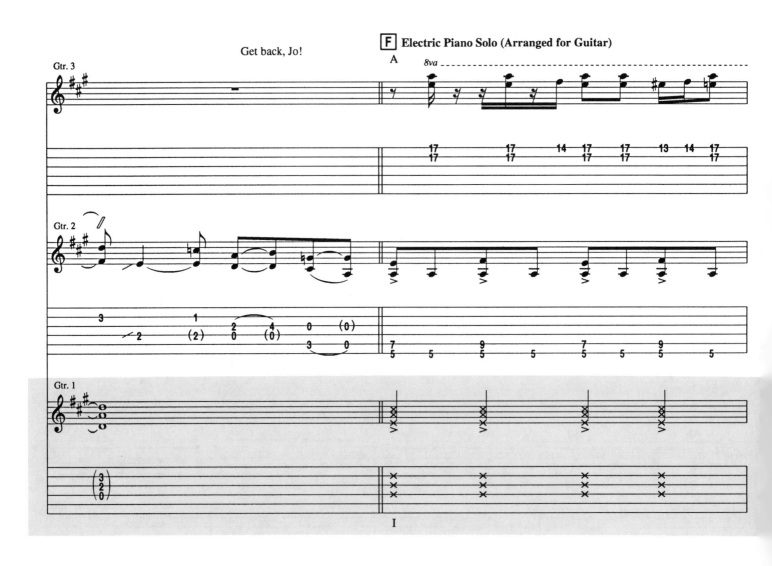

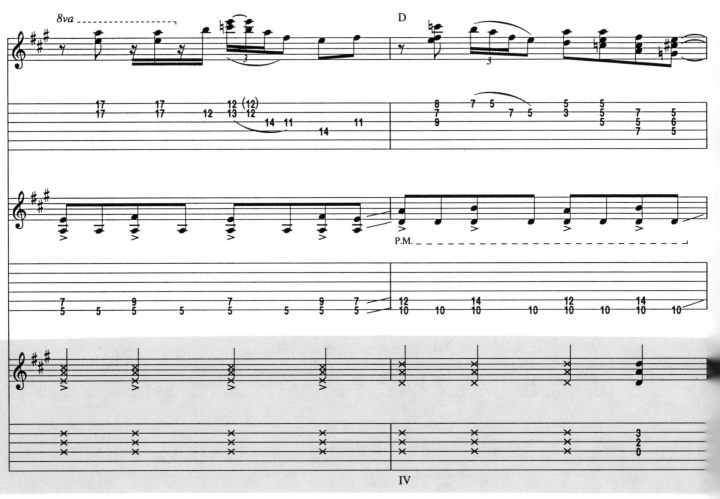

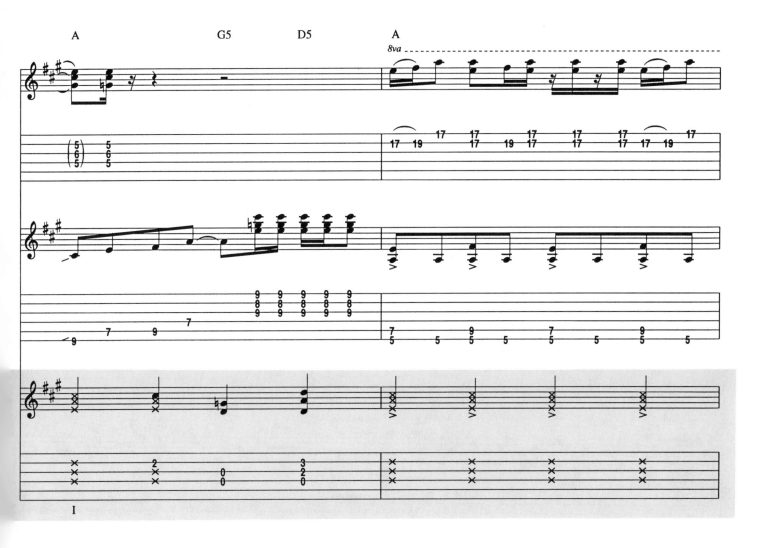

D.S. al Coda

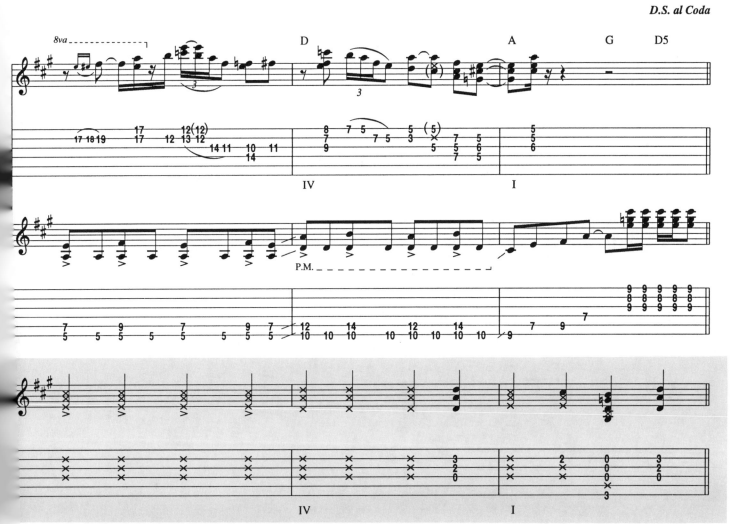

Coda

SCRATCH-N-SNIFF
Stevie Ray Vaughan

To play Stevie Ray Vaughan's music it will be necessary to tune a half-step lower to E♭. Get an E♭ note from a piano and then follow the relative tuning procedure in *Basics 1*: p. 6 or use an electronic tuner to get the pitches string by string. You can, of course, use the companion CD or cassette tape which has the tuning recorded and comparison tune by ear.

"Scratch-n-sniff" is built on a driving straight-eighth-note groove which splits the difference between blues and rock. It begins on the V chord in the key of A, E. (See *Basics 2*: p. 12.)

In the opening measures of the intro [A], Stevie plays a unison/open string riff which is a familiar blues-rock cliche and fairly simple to play.

In the verses [B], he lays down a strong comping figure made of A5–A6–A7 voicings based on the open A5 power chord (*Basics 1*: p. 45).

The second half of the verse rhythm part (bar 17) uses a movable blues comping figure in E (*Basics 2*: pp. 14-15).

These shapes and basic rhythmic idea are continued in the comping behind the guitar solo [C]. Here a IV–I–IV–V progression is found.

The solo is fairly simple but in its entirety is a little beyond the scope of *Basics 1*. Practice your open pentatonic scale fingerings and string bending in *Basics 1* as preparation. Try to tackle the solo only after you've gotten comfortable with those techniques. You'll be able to play it easily by the time you've mastered the movable lead guitar patterns from Chapter Four of *Basics 2*. Until then play along by sticking to the background comping and listening.

From the Epic recording IN STEP

Scratch-n-sniff

Words and Music by STEVIE RAY VAUGHAN and DOYLE BRAMHALL

Tune Down 1/2 Step
①= Eb ②= Bb
③= Gb ④= Db
⑤= Ab ⑥= Eb

A **Introduction**

Uptempo Rocker ♩ = 163

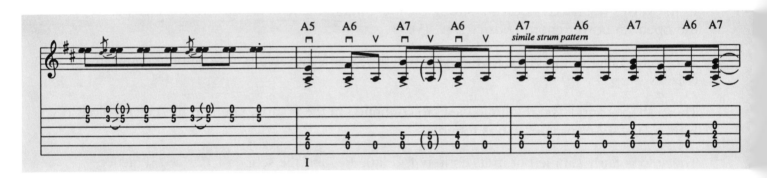

1. They were

 B **Verse**

two lone-ly folks — ah, do-in' the do's and don'ts, and got the no-tion to-geth-er they'd be hap -
2. ask-in' what if ____ they had to scratch 'n' sniff to find out what it is they are af -
3. on their _ side, they got noth-in' to hide. Nev-er had no se-crets be-tween them.

*Last note of guitar solo

- py.   Thought they'd lose   the crowd _ 'n' do the mess   a - round. _   De -
- ter.   Got the ants   out their pants 'n' took the chance   on ro-mance,   made some
                   He don't need   to ac - cuse her, use her, or   a - buse her,

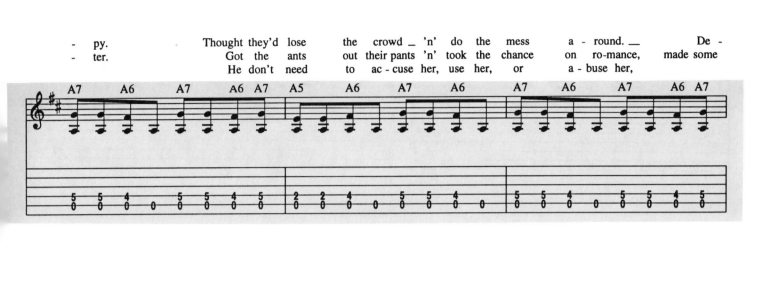

cid - ed   to make it snap - py.   Just a   twist   of fate _ they did - n't
plans   to make it for - ev - er.   Sev - 'ral   years   have gone, _ they're still
    and   she feel the same for him.   And those   vows   they made _ said noth - in'

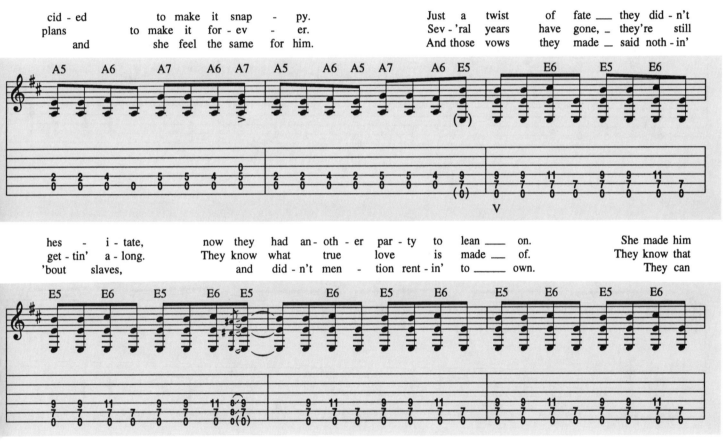

hes - i - tate,   now they had an - oth - er par - ty to lean _ on.   She made him
get - tin' a - long.   They know what   true   love is made _ of.   They know that
'bout slaves,   and did - n't men - tion rent - in' to _ own.   They can

jump   and sang, _ he made her share that   thang,   looks like _ they gon - na have   a ball. _
life's   a trip _ with all it's bumps and   dips.   They're gon - na help one an - oth - er a - long. _
take   the stand that walk - in' hand in   hand,   what they   got is good - er _ than gold. _

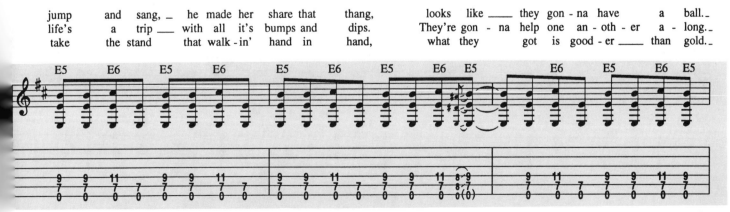

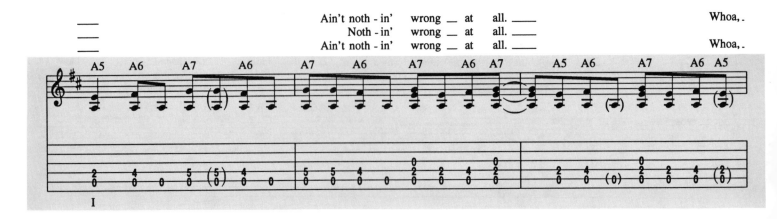

Ain't noth - in' wrong __ at all. ____   Whoa,.
Noth - in' wrong __ at all. ____   Whoa,.
Ain't noth - in' wrong __ at all. ____

To Coda ⊕

Piano Solo

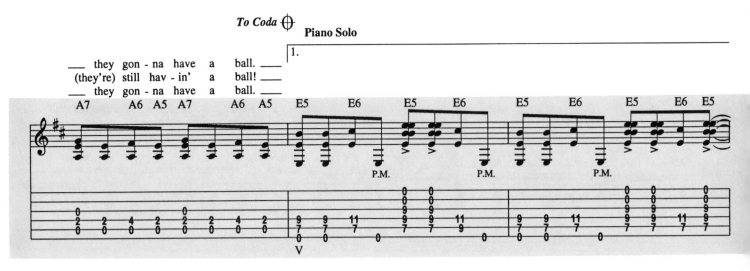

__ they gon - na have a ball. ____
(they're) still hav - in' a ball! ____
__ they gon - na have a ball. ____

1.

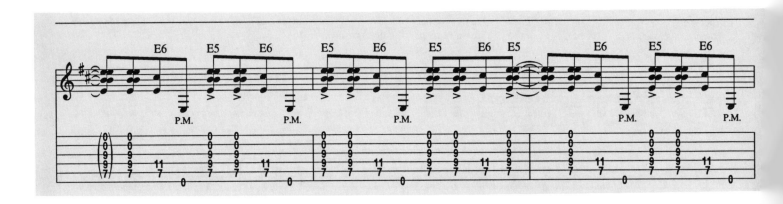

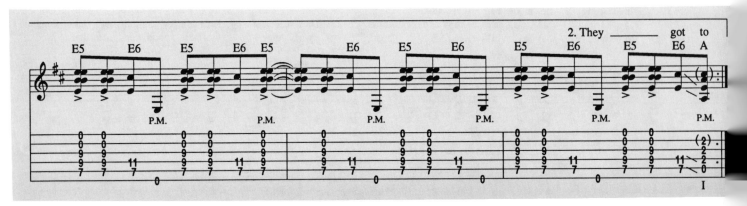

2. They ____ got to
A

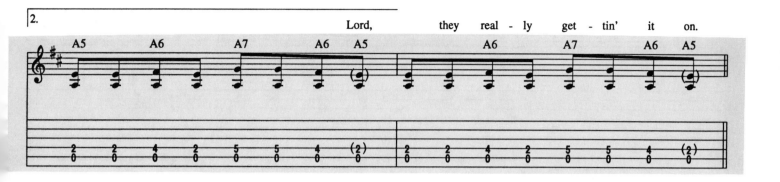

Lord,   they   real - ly   get - tin'   it   on.

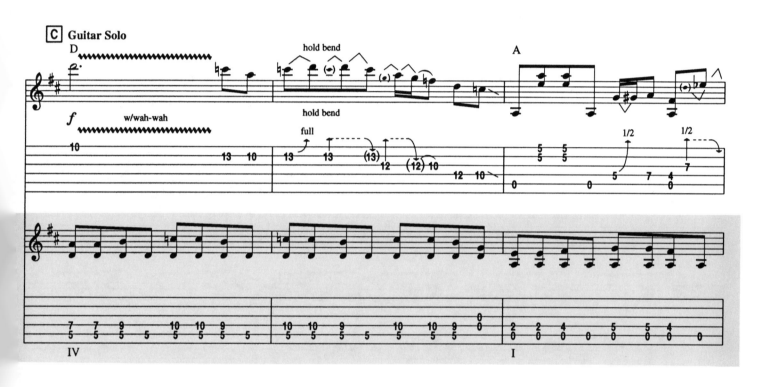

C Guitar Solo

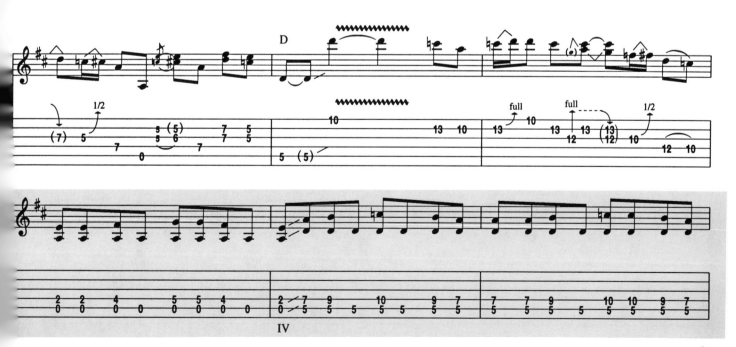

D.S. al Coda

3. Time is

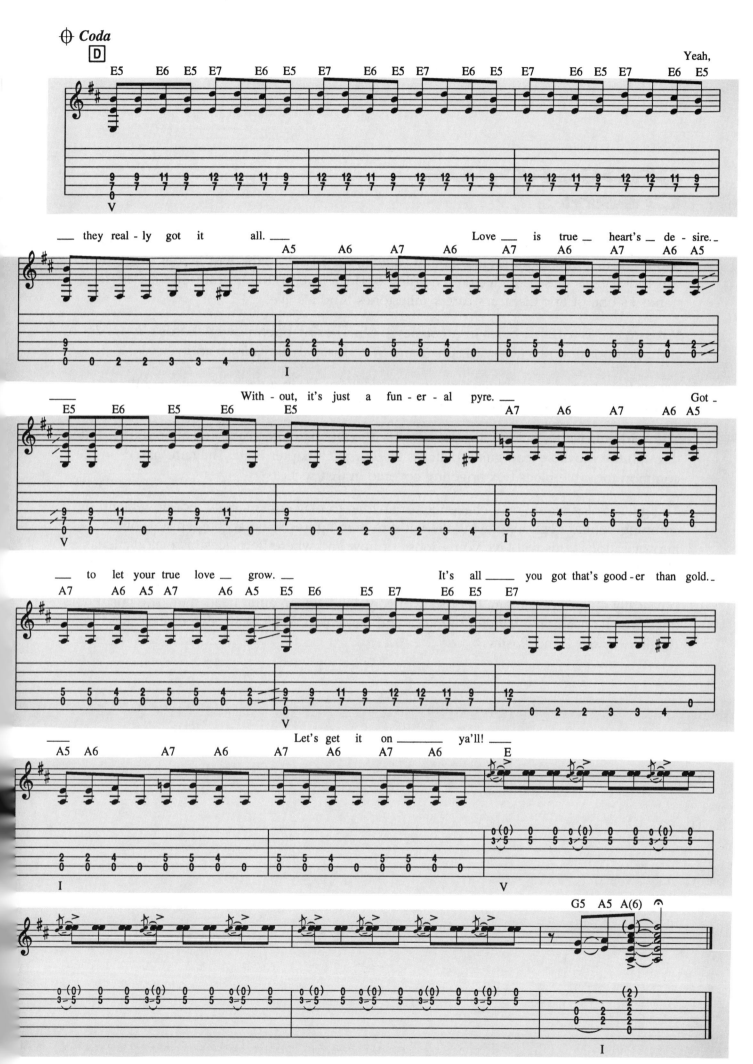

CROSSROADS
Cream

One of the greatest blues/rock guitar performances of all time, this track influenced droves of players from contemporaries like Jimmy Page and Jeff Beck to modern heroes like Edward Van Halen. This masterful electric rendering of Delta legend Robert Johnson's classic song stands as one of Eric Clapton's career milestones. And it's live!

"Crossroads" is a 12-bar blues in A (*Basics 1*: Ch. 4) using open power chords (*Basics 1*: Ch. 2) and open position riffs (*Basics 1*: Ch. 3 and 5) consistently in its intro and verses.

Notice the open position blues comping (*Basics 1*: p. 37) in a well-accented eighth-note groove and palm-muting (*Basics 1*: p. 27) throughout the verses.

The lead guitar lines in the intro [A], bars 10-12, will be quite accessible after you've gotten through the movable lead guitar patterns in *Basics 2*, Chapter Four. They are based on the common movable blues box fingering covered in that section.

The guitar solos would be a challenge for anyone to play convincingly. For now begin by comping behind Clapton; playing the verse rhythm figures as an accompanist to his improvisations. This will give you a sense of how and where he places his melodic ideas rhythmically and harmonically and get you to listen to the overall effect first. If you keep up this practice you will be very familiar with the sound and feel of the lines by the time you're physically able to play them. In other words, you'll have an aural head start. The guitar solo lines are all based on a handful of minor and major pentatonic scale shapes explained in detail in *Basics 2* and *Basics 3*.

From the RSO recording WHEELS OF FIRE

Crossroads

Words and Music by Robert Johnson

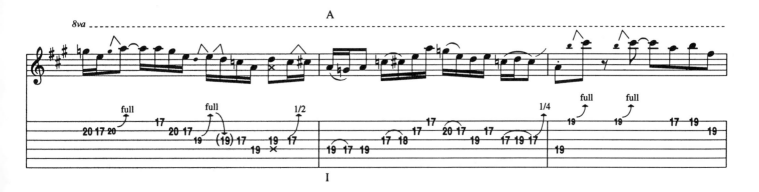

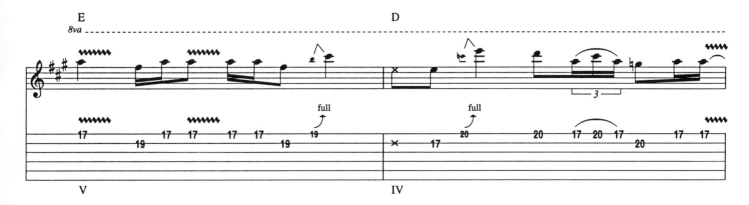

D.S. al Coda 2

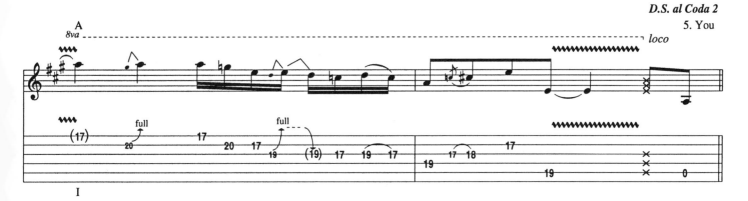

5. You

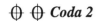

Coda 2

lieve I'm sinkin' down.

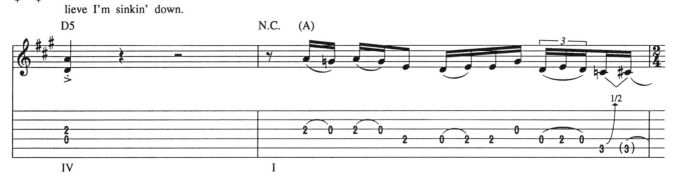

Free time

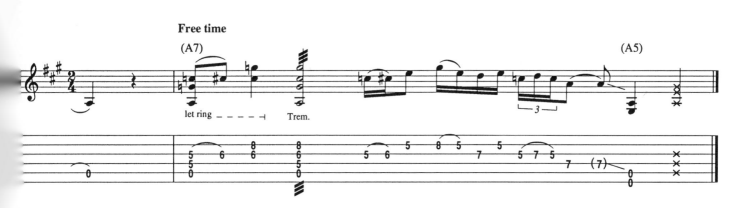

THE UNFORGIVEN
Metallica

This powerful and moody Metallica song is from their eponymously-titled 1991 release which was something of a breakthrough record for the band—commercially and artistically. In this release they broadened their style by adding overt melodicism and simpler grooves to the typically hard and heavy thrash approach of their earlier efforts. "The Unforgiven" is a perfect example of what modern metal is all about. Filled with contrasts of texture, dynamics, orchestration and mood, it is truly one of Metallica's finest moments.

In this arrangement there is a lot of labeling of figures, fills and riffs. Refer back to the glossary explanation if you need additional information.

The intro [A] begins with an acoustic guitar (Gtr. 1) playing a sixteenth-note arpeggiation that is fingerpicked. (See *Basics 2*: p. 56 for more on fingerpicking.) The part is built on an open A5 power chord (*Basics 1*: Ch. 2) and its related open A minor chord (*Basics 2*: p. 49). Visualize the close relationship between the open A5 and Am shapes. Gtr. 2 enters at [B]. This is a simple melody played on a clean electric guitar. This uncomplicated line should be easy to play by the time you've gotten half way through *Basics 1*. However it uses finger vibrato consistently. (Refer to *Basics 2*: Ch. 4 if you need to know more about this technique.)

This quiet mood gives way to a crushing metal groove in the verses [C], Rhy. Fig. 3. Check out this section for open power chords: A5, E5 and D5 (*Basics 1*: Ch. 1) and palm-muting (*Basics 1*: p. 27). Power chords and palm-muting may well be the common denominator of all hard rock and metal music.

In the choruses [D] things calm down a bit and a variant of the simple intro melody is heard in the Gtr. 2 line. Play the fingerpicked arpeggiation of Rhy. Fig. 5 behind the lead guitar lines in the interlude [E] for now. Listen and after you've gotten familiar with the sound and feel of those lines against the chord make your first attempts to learn the Gtr. 2 part.

Similarly, play Rhy. Fig. 3 behind the guitar solo at [F]. These solo licks will be physically within your reach by the time you get through *Basics 3* and are ready for *Advanced Concepts and Techniques*. (In that volume, the modal scales and special techniques that Kirk Hammett is using are thoroughly explained.)

In the outro [G], play the Gtr. 1 part, Rhy. Fig. 6, behind the melody. This rhythm figure is comprised of simple open chords covered in *Basics 2*, Chapter 5. Again, after you have the feel and sound in your ear, then and only then begin to focus on the lead guitar melody lines.

The Unforgiven

Words and Music by James Hetfield, Lars Ulrich and Kirk Hammett

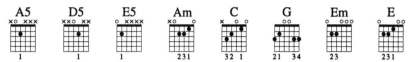

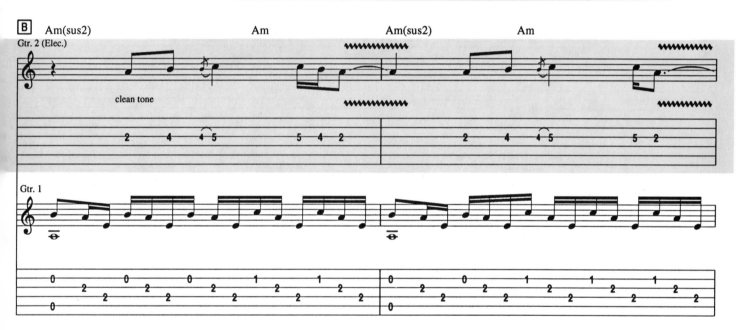

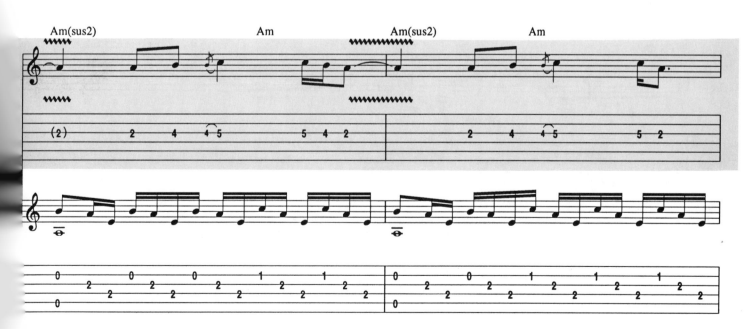

Through constant pain, disgrace, the young boy learns their rules.
He tries to please disgrace, them all, young this bitter man he is.

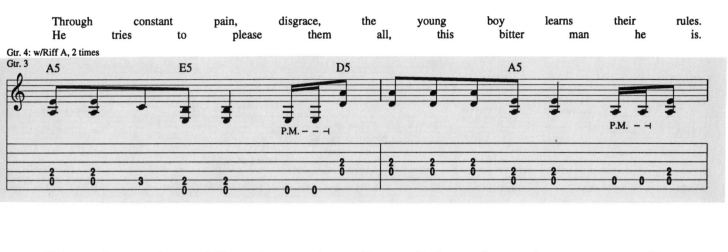

With time, the child draws in this whipping boy done wrong. De -
Throughout his life draws the same, he's boy battled constantly. This

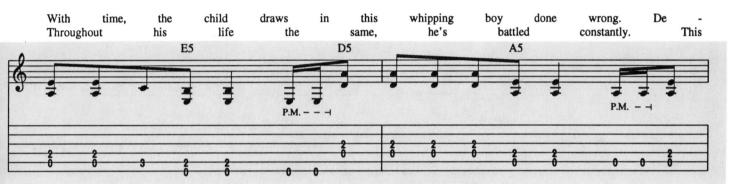

prived of all his thoughts the young man struggles on and on. He's known, oo, a
fight he cannot win. A tired man they see no longer cares. The

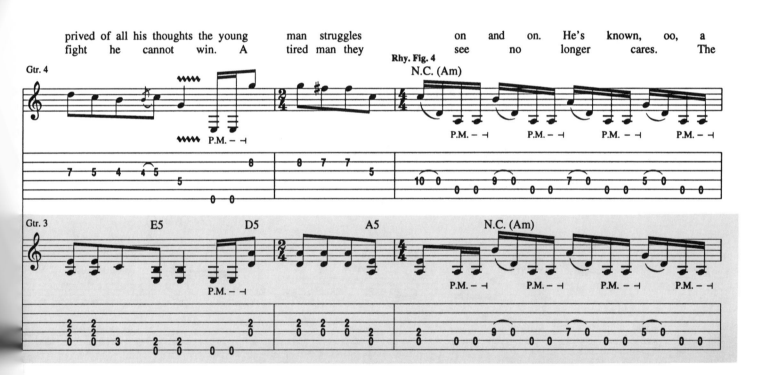

vow unto his own that never from this day his will they'll take away.
old man then prepares to die regretfully. That old man here is me.

Gtr. 1: w/Rhy. Fig. 1, 2 times

𝄋 D Chorus

What I've felt, what I've known, never shined through in what I've

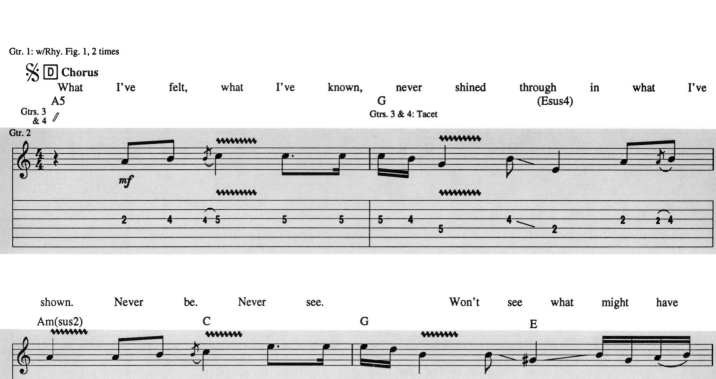

shown. Never be. Never see. Won't see what might have

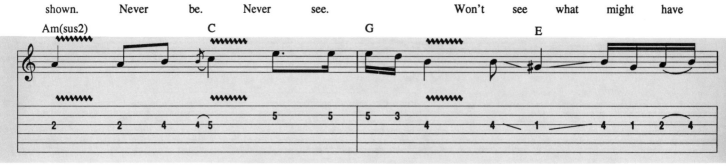

been. What I've felt, what I've known never shined through in what I've shown.

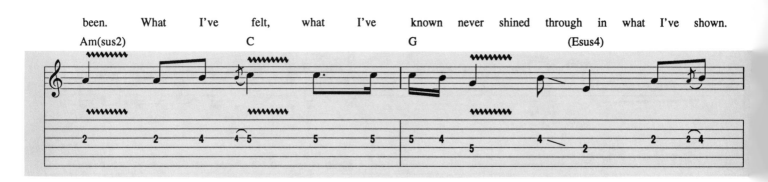

To Coda ⊕

Never free. Never me. So I dub thee unforgiven.

Gtr. 1: w/Rhy. Fig. 2

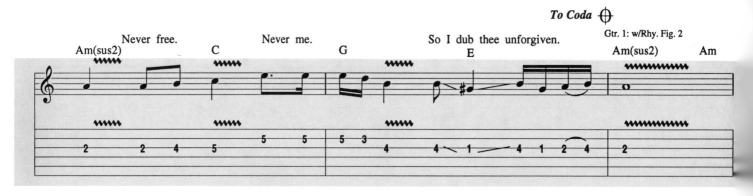

76

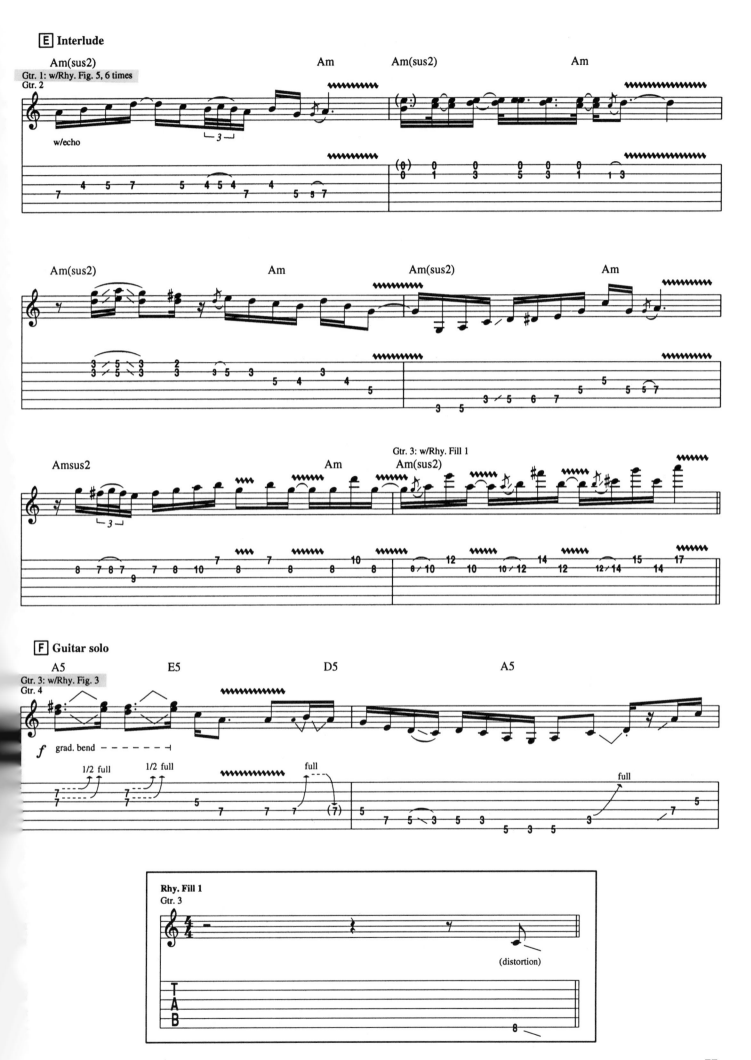

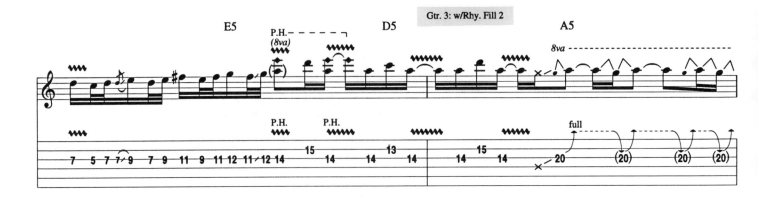

Gtr. 3: w/Rhy. Fig. 3

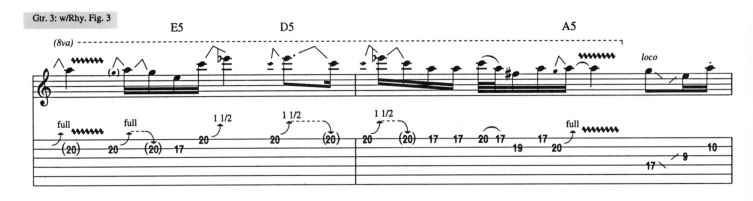

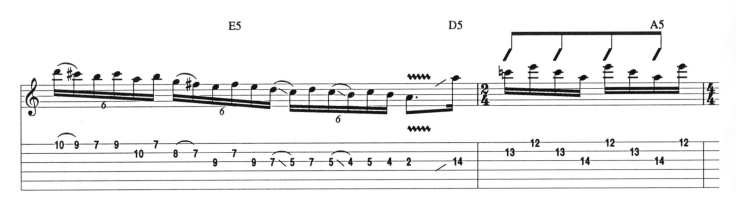

Gtr. 3: w/Rhy. Fig. 4

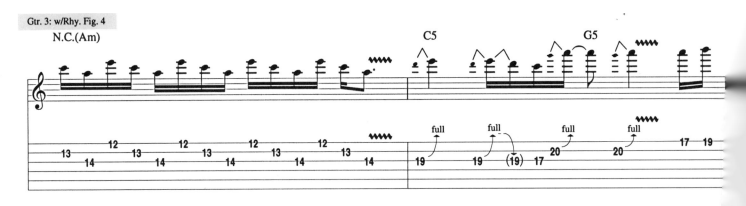

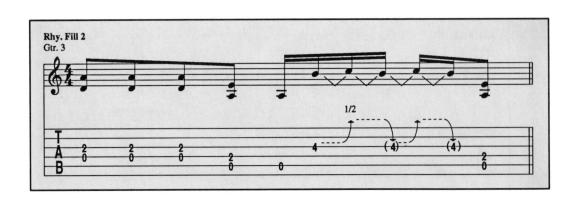

Rhy. Fill 2
Gtr. 3

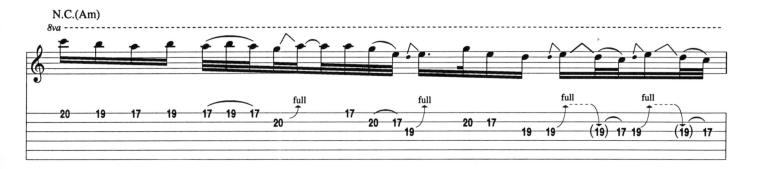

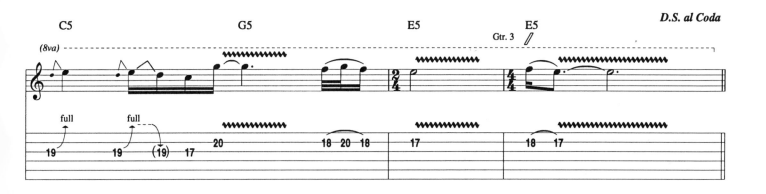

D.S. al Coda

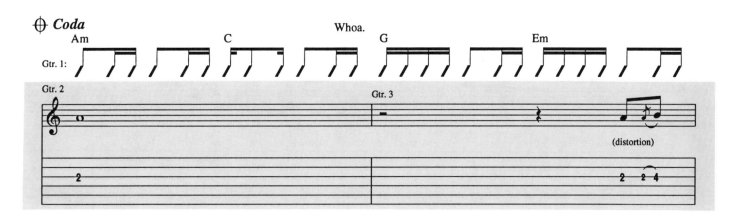

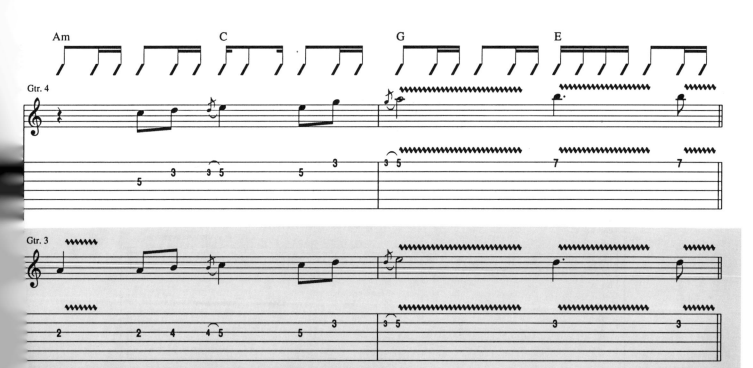

G Outro

Never free. Never me. So I dub thee unforgiven.

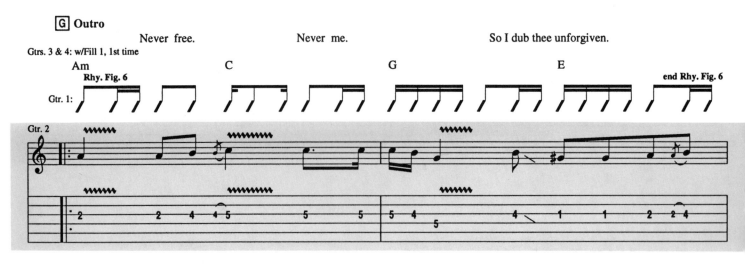

Gtrs. 3 & 4: w/Riff B, to end
Gtr. 1: w/Rhy. Fig. 6, to end

You labeled me. I'll label you.

So I dub thee unforgiven. *Repeat and Fade*

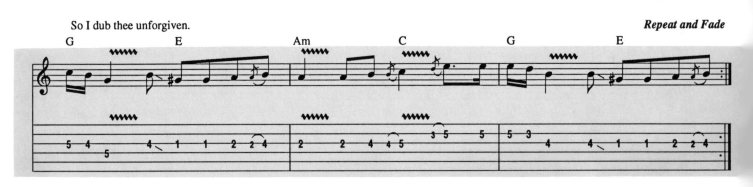

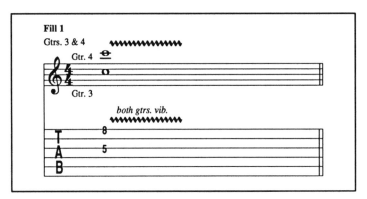

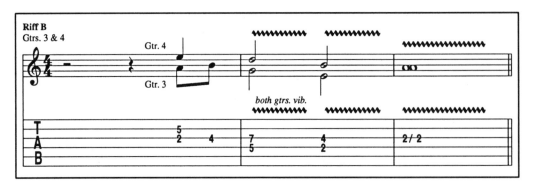

BOOT HILL
Stevie Ray Vaughan

Stevie Ray Vaughan supercharges this traditional blues composition with his aggressive blues-rock approach and a fiery debut on electric slide guitar. Before you start, tune your guitar to Eb, a half-step below standard concert pitch. (See the suggestions in "Scratch-n-sniff".) The form is a standard 12-bar blues in E (*Basics 1*: Ch. 4) and the piece is set in a driving shuffle groove (*Basics 1*: p. 39).

Throughout the verses, Stevie employs fifth-to-sixth blues comping (*Basics 1*: pp. 37-39) as the rhythm riff on E, the I chord, and A, the IV chord. Visualize their related open power chord shapes (*Basics 1*: Ch. 1) as you strum the comping pattern. The open B7 is a simple partial chord form (*Basics 2*: p. 61) which is arpeggiated and added to the progression as the V chord.

Now about the slide guitar lines. Here are some basics:

1. Wear the slide on your pinky so that you can still comp rhythm comfortably with the other fingers. When playing slide guitar, don't press the slide down with pressure on the strings. Rather let it glide lightly from note to note while making firm contact with the string surface.

2. Use fret-hand muting with the index, ring or middle finger(s) behind the slide to silence any unwanted string noise created by the slide. And believe me, there will be plenty, especially with a distorted electric guitar tone.

3. Be conscious of sliding into notes—don't try to hit them dead on as if fretting.

4. Think of slide guitar as constantly tuning while you play—so listen and keep checking the intonation of your lines.

5. When sliding into notes remember that, unlike normal guitar playing, you must stop the string directly above a fret—not behind it—to sound the proper pitch.

6. When using vibrato move the slide along the string surface—don't try to bend the string as in standard string bending vibrato.

Begin by learning the immortal slide cliche in the intro [A]. This is basically just a repeated diad on the high E and B strings. It's played in a fairly consistent eighth-note rhythm so it should be easy to grasp with a minimum of practice. From there, go ahead and tackle the solo [C]. Once you've mastered the basic technique and have the intro under your belt, these should present no unusual problems. If they do, listen while comping the verse rhythm figures behind the solo. Repeat this practice regularly. With familiarity these lines will be within your reach.

Boot Hill

Arranged and Adapted by Stevie Ray Vaughan

Tune Down 1/2 Step

①= E♭ ②= B♭
③= G♭ ④= D♭
⑤= A♭ ⑥= E♭

A Intro

Medium Blues Shuffle (♩. = 96)

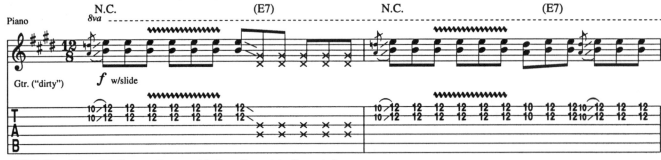

NOTE: Wear slide on little finger to allow normal fretting with remaining fingers during verse.

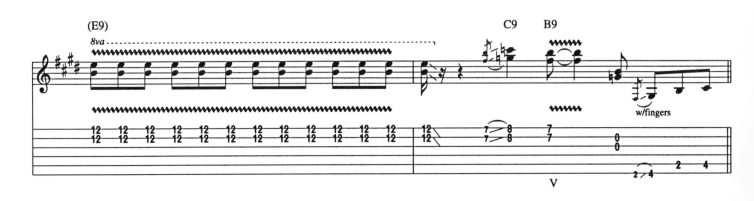

B Verse

1. Look up on the wall, baby   hand me down   my   shootin' iron.

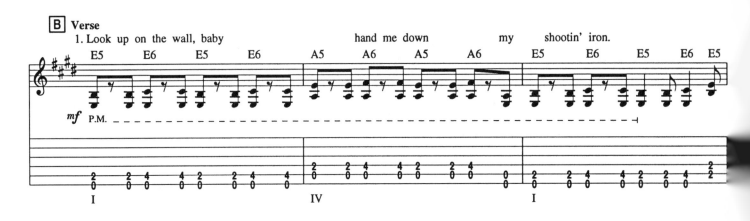

Look up on the wall, baby   hand me down my

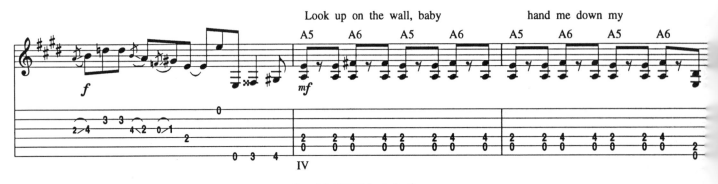

you're goin' way out on   that boot hill.

D Guitar Solo

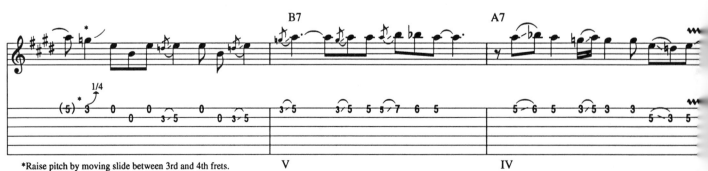

*Raise pitch by moving slide between 3rd and 4th frets.

GLOSSARY

There are a number of important and useful musical terms, abbreviations and stylistic elements found in modern guitar transcriptions and arrangements. So that it will be easier for you to negotiate your way through the Power Studies songs, the following list and explanations are offered.

1. RIFF. In a general sense, this is synonymous with repeated figure. A riff is normally a self-contained and sonically identifiable musical idea. In a song form sense, it has a more specific meaning. It means a recurring figure or pattern which is structurally important to the arrangement. It is used to describe a mostly single-note figure or one that is more melodic than chordal. Multiple riffs in a song are given letter names to distinguish one from the other. For example, Riff A, Riff B, Riff C and so on. It is named when it first appears so that it may be recalled throughout the arrangement.

2. RHYTHM FIGURE. This is the converse of riff. Rhythm Figure refers to a recurring pattern which is more chordal than melodic. It can be a purely strummed part, a series of arpeggiated chords, triads, an intricate progression or something as simple as just a repeating diad. Multiple rhythm figures in a song are abbreviated and given numbers in an arrangement. For example, Rhy. Fig. 1, Rhy. Fig. 2 and so on.

3. TACET. This means don't play in a particular section of a song. When you have several bars of tacet, it is written as long, thick whole-note rest with brackets on each end. The number above the rest tells you how many measures to remain silent.

4. GUITARS. In arrangements with more than one guitar, they are given proper guitar part names, abbreviated and numbered. For example, Gtr. 1, Gtr. 2, etc. If there is something significant about the particular Gtr. part it will usually be cited. For example, acoustic or electric guitar, clean, semi-clean (semi-cln.) or distorted (dirty) tone, etc. Particular articulations are also cited: let ring, P.M., with fingers and pick, with slide, etc. Effects which significantly process the sound are similarly designated: with echo, with fuzz, with flanger, etc.

5. SONG FORM. Here are some basic musical symbols, terms and points used to set up the structure of a song as an arrangement.

REPEAT MARKS. These are written as bracketed sections with thick barlines on the outside and thin barlines on the inside. These are followed by two vertical dots. If they are repeated more than once, the direction is written as a number of times. For example, these symbols

mean repeat the inside two bars (play them twice) and then continue. If you played them again (three times) it would be written with this added direction

Play 3 times

First, second, third (etc.) endings are used with longer repeat sections if their final few bars have different music. For example these symbols

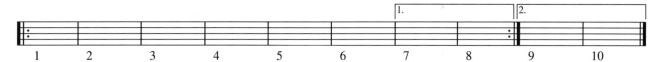

mean that you are dealing with an eight bar section which has different music in the last two bars on the repeat. Play the first eight bars (1-8), repeat only the first six bars (1-6) before going on to the second ending (bars 9-10) to complete the eight-bar section.

D.S. (DAL SEGNO). This literally means "from the sign". You'll see it accompanied by this symbol:

It is used to indicate the beginning of a section to be repeated. The abbreviation D.S. means go to the sign and repeat until a new direction is given or until the music ends. D.S. is usually found with the words Al Coda. And no, Al Coda is not a famous Italian musician. D.S. Al Coda means "from the sign, go to the coda".

CODA. This literally means "the tail" and refers to a concluding section of a piece of music. You'll see it written with this symbol:

Inside these broad mappings of the arrangement, you will find the various song form sections labelled. These could include:

INTRO (Introduction). VERSES (1st Verse, 2nd Verse, etc.). PRE-CHORUS. CHORUS. INTERLUDE. BRIDGE. SOLO (or solos). OUTRO (ending section).

6. FILL. This is a brief melodic figure inserted into the arrangement. These are often boxed, named and numbered. For example, Fill 1, Fill 2, etc. When these are brought into the song they are called up by the direction: w/Fill 1, w/Fill 2, etc.

7. RHYTHM FILL. This is a chordal version of the Fill. It can be an independent little figure or a piece of a larger Rhy. Fig. These are also boxed, named and numbered. When named they are abbreviated. For example, Rhy. Fill 1, Rhy. Fill 2, etc. They are called up just like Fills, by the direction: w/Rhy. Fill 1, w/Rhy. Fill 2, etc.

8. RHYTHM SLASHES. These are strum symbols written as rhythm patterns with chord names located above the staff. When you see these, look for corresponding chord frames in the beginning of the arrangement. Find the name that goes with the frame. They will show you, in diagram form, the chords to be played. For example, this

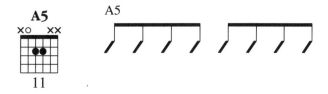

means you play the A5 chord shown in the frame with a steady eighth-note strum. Articulations like P.M. and x's are often included and appear below the rhythm pattern. Rhythm slashes can also indicate single notes in a figure. In this case, the rhythm pattern will show note heads instead of strum slashes. The note name will appear above rhythm pattern, followed by its fret number and string number.

NOTATION LEGEND